P9-EDC-333

PS
3553
A4
Z87
1993

147148

N.L. TERTELING LIBRARY
ALBERTSON COLLEGE
CALDWELL, IDAHO

PURCHASED WITH NEH
ENDOWMENT FUNDS

The Fiction
of Hortense Calisher

The Fiction
of Hortense Calisher

Kathleen Snodgrass

DELAWARE

Newark: University of Delaware Press
London and Toronto: Associated University Presses

PS 3553
A4
Z 87
1993

© 1993 by Associated University Presses, Inc.

All rights reserved. Authorization to photocopy items for internal or personal use, or the internal or personal use of specific clients, is granted by the copyright owner, provided that a base fee of $10.00, plus eight cents per page, per copy is paid directly to the Copyright Clearance Center, 27 Congress Street, Salem, Massachusetts 01970. [0-87413-478-1/93 $10.00 + 8¢ pp, pc.]

Associated University Presses
440 Forsgate Drive
Cranbury, NJ 08512

Associated University Presses
25 Sicilian Avenue
London WC1A 2QH, England

Associated University Presses
P.O. Box 338, Port Credit
Mississauga, Ontario
Canada L5G 4L8

The paper used in this publication meets the requirements of the American National Standard for Permanence of Paper for Printed Library Materials Z39.48-1984.

Library of Congress Cataloging-in-Publication Data

Snodgrass, Kathleen, 1950–
    The fiction of Hortense Calisher / Kathleen Snodgrass.
        p.   cm.
    Includes bibliographical references and index.
    ISBN 0-87413-478-1 (alk. paper)
    1. Calisher, Hortense—Criticism and interpretation.   I. Title.
PS3553.A4Z87   1993
813'.54—dc20   92-50667
                                                         CIP

PRINTED IN THE UNITED STATES OF AMERICA

147148

For De

N. L. TERTELING LIBRARY
ALBERTSON COLLEGE OF IDAHO
CALDWELL, ID 83605

But veritable travelers are the ones who leave
For leaving's sake; with hearts as light as balloon
They go; their destiny is clear; they never swerve,
Forever calling out, they don't know why: Come on!
                    —"Le Voyage" (Baudelaire)

Contents

Acknowledgments

Quotations from *Age* and *Kissing Cousins* by Hortense Calisher are reprinted by permission of Grove Weidenfeld, New York. Quotations from all other works by Calisher are reprinted by permission of Donadio and Ashworth, Inc., New York. Copyright © 1993 by Hortense Calisher.

An earlier version of chapter 2 originally appeared as an essay titled "Coming Down from Heights: Three Novels of Hortense Calisher" in *Texas Studies in Literature and Language* 31, no. 4 (Winter 1989), pp. 445–569, reprinted by permission of the University of Texas Press.

The translation of Charles Baudelaire's poem "Le Voyage" is acknowledged by the following credit line:

Charles Baudelaire. "The Journey," copyright © 1991 by William H. Crosby. Reprinted from *The Flowers of Evil & Paris Spleen*, by Charles Baudelaire, translated by William H. Crosby, with the permission of BOA Editions, Ltd., 92 Park Ave., Brockport, NY 14420.

The Fiction
of Hortense Calisher

Introduction

Hortense Calisher, known primarily as a "writer's writer," has been turning out works of serious fiction for over forty years. Her eleven novels, six collections of short stories and novellas, and two autobiographical works have been consistently, sometimes lengthily, reviewed; she has served as president of American PEN and of the American Academy and Institute of Arts and Letters and has been the recipient of two Guggenheims and, more recently, an NEA Senior Fellowship. But despite her reputation as a significant voice in American fiction she has received neither popular acclaim nor, excepting two doctoral dissertations, in-depth critical analyses. The absence of the first is understandable enough: Calisher's dense and quirky fictions are not the stuff of which bestsellers are made. Reasons for the critical silence are less easy to come by. One possibility lies in the resistance of her works to easy categorization: she is not, in any narrow sense, a woman's writer, a Jewish writer, or a New York writer. She is, however, a writer known for her distinctive, even idiosyncratic, style. Especially when surveying Calisher's career, reviewers single out her style—usually summed up as "convoluted," "elliptical," or "Jamesian"—as the one constant. They rarely situate a new novel within Calisher's canon, let alone within the context of contemporary fiction. As a result, each new work seems, notwithstanding its stylistic signature, *sui generis*.

It is certainly true, as a number of her reviewers have remarked, that Calisher's subject matter covers a vast range of territory. Yet however varied the novels' imaginative worlds, a thematic continuity exists that, for too long, has gone unnoticed. It was not until a 1987 *Paris Review* interview that Calisher, recalling the unique physical sensation of her childhood's trolley rides, referred to that theme's presence in her fiction:

> That reversal—how it could in effect turn that huge, lumbering car the other way around—gave me pause even then. Maybe transportation as a theme of mine started then. It's the opposite of a firm sense of place—or of a yearning for the true place.[1]

11

For over forty years Calisher has spun out variations on that theme: her protagonists may yearn for if not the true place then at least a firmly manageable one in which to stay put, but by novel's or novella's end, they come out into a world that promises not a safe place, but an open-ended journey. That reviewers have failed to grasp that theme's all-pervasiveness—the thematic centrality of, simultaneously, rites of passage and of extradition—only underscores her achievement. That they have failed to see that style is not something imposed on subject matter, but, rather, the perfect vehicle for and embodiment of her life's theme, has resulted in an unfortunate stereotyping of Calisher the consummate stylist.

Calisher's impressive range, the variousness of story, character and structure, have vitalized a theme which, by nature of its very universality, could easily have conjured up cliché upon cliché. This study sets out to examine not only that theme's dominance in Calisher's work but also its many variations.

It seems especially fitting that Calisher should locate that theme's objective correlative in a childhood memory; her own upbringing provided rich material for her earliest stories. Hortense Calisher was born on 20 December 1911 in New York City, the first of two children born to Joseph Calisher, a Richmond-born Jew, and Hedwig Lichstern Calisher, a German Jewish émigré twenty-two years her husband's junior. Looking back at her childhood, Calisher has observed that the conflicts in her household—of generation, class, heritage, and, temperament—were "bound to produce someone interested in character, society, and time."[2]

It wasn't until she was in her late thirties that Calisher wrote the first of a dozen autobiographical stories. Her heroine, Hester Elkin, is a perennially gawky, bookish child, the despair of her beautiful, demanding, and utterly prosaic mother. Her manufacturer father, a *fin de siècle* dandy in his youth, is an autodidact who reads both Hebrew and German with a drawl. The paternal portrait that emerges from Calisher's autobiographical stories and from her memoir, *Herself,* is of a man who attends as much to the art of living well as to the demands of making a living. His wife, on the other hand, views his *joie de vivre* as a dangerously frivolous quality; her husband and his family genuinely baffle her, for "somewhere along the line they have become incapable of caring most about money" (*H,* 61).[3]

While the autobiographical stories accentuate the differences of experience and of sensibility, Calisher evokes another, more congenial atmosphere in a *Mademoiselle* article originally entitled "My Life as a Female Sex Object" (which the magazine saccharinely retitled "The Pride and Joy of Growing Up a Woman"). Calisher describes the atmosphere peculiar to her household that imbued her with an enviable self-confidence:

> The main fact about our household was that it had been founded on a departure from the sexual norm. An "old" man—in his fifties—had married a girl in her twenties. . . . [S]ocial innuendo from without and family comment from within made it clear to me early on that I was the product of a special desire on somebody's part. . . . My father made it plain that this somebody was particularly him. Also that we children, as latecomers and intensely craved ones, are glamorously special too.[4]

The spacious apartment itself was "glamorously special," full of "genteel porn"; forks, sugar bowls, pipes, brushes, letter openers—even the hatrack—were adorned with female nudes:

> As the social psychologists . . . might say: "Your parents taught you sexual health sublimally." All the more amazing then, since they taught me to worry about so much else. Financial hypochondria was my mother's speciality. My father had a biblical fear which all his ebullience couldn't conceal; no one could convince him that he and those he loved weren't going to die. . . . How lucky for me then, that certain other household clues . . . would seem to be murmuring spiritedly "Lots of sex here, before you go."[5]

Along the way, Calisher imbibed another important message:

> we had brains. Many healthy families feel the same, but our preening had a sleeper in it which was to serve me very well; women were assumed to have the same brainpower as men.[6]

However different her parents were, "between them they created a household . . . both sensual and satiric, in which both flesh and mind were given their sometimes due."[7]

Her father had a "'small but representative collection'" of books and Calisher read voraciously, from Boccaccio to the Bible—the book Calisher cites as having had the greatest impact on her writing.[8] From an early age, the city was her teacher as well; by age ten she had "been shallowly tutored in music and dance" and was soon haunting museums, theaters, and concert halls:

> I am not learning "art." I am being taught an attitude, that art is necessary. And who but the city is teaching me—that the arts are at the same time holy and plebian, expensive and cheap? Or that art interest . . . is ordinary gospel here. Shortly, when I come to want to be an artist myself, the city itself will rise in me like a great pulse.[9]

In the heart of the Depression, Calisher "came out" (*H, 20*) to college, work, and marriage. While her mother was determined that her daughter would find secretarial work after graduating from high school, Calisher had other plans and just the right strategy to realize them:

> Pride of my dancing school, I went and got the chorus job guaranteed to blow my mother's cool—and me, of course, to sexual ruin. "I start on Monday," I said. So, to college I went. (*H, 18*)

After earning an A.B. from Barnard in 1932, with a major in English and a minor in Philosophy, she worked as an investigator for the Department of Public Welfare:

> I was projected into that great part of life you would never have seen from the confines of a proper home and the proper schools. This made some rather deep changes in me; I began to have some small insight into social thinking.[10]

In 1935 she married a newly-degreed engineer, Heaton Bennet Heffelfinger, by whom she had two children, Bennet and Peter. For thirteen years, Calisher was a full-time wife and mother, living in a series of "American provinces" (*H, 31*):

> As a New Yorker I am out of it in one way, as a Jew in another (almost all engineers at this time were, like my husband, Christian). And as a secret artist . . . in a third way, perhaps the most significant. (*H, 28*)

Like the fictional counterpart in her 1953 story, "The Rabbi's Daughter," a gifted young pianist, now uprooted New Yorker, wife and mother, Calisher found neither the time nor the energy for writing,

> except for those poems, flung off in brief single seizures, in trances of regret for the intellectual life I seemed to have lost. I never sent the poems out. I am paralyzed, not only by the house-and-child life—which is a total-flesh-draining, a catatonia of rest for the beaverish brain, that in a way is craved—but by this immersion in a society where I feel . . . ultimately lunatic-wrong. (*H, 29*)

Eventually, however, "Hoards of selfhood . . . had to find their spill-way" (*H, 39*). Calisher began writing the first of her autobiographical stories—or, rather, while walking her son to school mornings, composed it in her head. This first story, published in 1948, was followed in quick succession by others. By 1951 she had published thirteen, predominantly autobiographical, stories, seven of which appeared in *The New Yorker*.

The decade that followed (1951–1961) was an eventful one for Calisher: her collection of short stories, *In the Absence of Angels* (1951), established her reputation as a fully-developed talent. Her stories appeared regularly in magazines, and she became a contributor of essays and reviews to *The Reporter*. In 1952 and 1955 Calisher went to England on Guggenheim fellowships and in 1958 to Southeast Asia on a Department of State American Specialists grant. Divorced in the late-fifties, Calisher taught for a semester at the Iowa Writers' Workshop, where she met the writer Curtis Harnack: "I had not come to meet a lover—the lover. Because the face is handsome, I even wisecrack to myself like a smart chorine—'Uh-*uh*, Hortense. No.' The last time I say it" (*H*, 123). They married in 1959.

> By this time [Calisher relates in *Herself*] I had passed through my fear of not being a writer, and of not finding a lover. Now I would have to pass through my fear of being a woman writer. Which by this time had less and less to do with the external limits dealt us, or the statuses. The real danger had always been that it would restrict what I wrote. . . . The real limits of art are always self-imposed. (*H*, 245)

Any fears she had were surely allayed by her own prodigious and varied output in the sixties. Like Colette, a writer Calisher much admires, she soon realized that she, too,

> is no more essentially feminine as a writer than any man is essentially masculine as a writer. . . . She uses the psychological and concrete dossiers in her possession as a woman, not only without embarassment but with the most natural sense of its value, and without any confusion as to whether the sexual balance of her sensitivity need affect the virility of her expression when she wants virility there. (*H*, 119)

The early, autobiographical stories established Calisher's reputation, yet once she had, in her own mind, exhausted that vein, she—like the prototypical Calisher protagonist—moved on, "out, to the wider world" (*H*, 42). In the sixties, Calisher published novels and novellas as well as non-autobiographical stories. Her first novel, *False Entry* (1961), a densely-textured exploration of one man's consciousness, mystified or simply irritated many reviewers who, it would seem, had neatly categorized her as a *New Yorker* writer. Two years later, Calisher published *Textures of Life* (1963). A far less ambitious work than *False Entry*, it quietly dramatizes a young Bohemian couple's passage from rebellion to accommodation. Two years later Calisher again demonstrated that, for her, eluding expectations was the rule rather than the exception: *Journal from Ellipsia* (1965) is a dazzling *tour de force*, the journal of an other-worldly creature struggling towards humanness. In 1969 Calisher published *The New Yorkers*, an expansive social drama and companion novel to *False Entry*.

The sixties also saw, interspersed among these novels, the publication of four novellas and two collections of short stories. Since the publication of her first novel, Calisher has generally alternated long works with short works, finding that the "'diversity energizes'" her (*Saturday Review* July/Aug. 1985: 77). A year after *False Entry* appeared, *Tale for the Mirror: A Novella and Other Stories* (1962) was published. This and the novellas that soon followed—*Extreme Magic* (1964), *The Railway Police* and *The Last Trolley Ride* (1966)—were further demonstrations of Calisher's imaginative range and power.

Calisher's seventies' novels—*Queenie* (1971), *Standard Dreaming* (1972), *Eagle Eye* (1973), and *On Keeping Women* (1977)—stylistically break new ground. The subjects themselves are commonplace: the coming-of-age of young adults in *Queenie* and *Eagle Eye,* midlife reevaluations in *Standard Dreaming* and *On Keeping Women*. There is nothing commonplace about Calisher's stylistic verve, her radical shifts of voice and perspective.

Although most reviewers highly praised Calisher's *Collected Stories* (1975), they did so for widely disparate, even contrary, reasons. Robert Phillips characterizes her

> story lines [as] often fragile, if not nonexistent. This is because in her fiction incident is subordinate to insight. The landscape is more often than not a psychescape of the protagonists.[11]

Eugenie Bolger writes that Calisher "believes in firm structures and plots. Her stories are filled with the detail that establishes mood and place."[12]

In 1983 Calisher published *Mysteries of Motion,* in terms of structure and scale, her most ambitious novel to date. She followed it, in 1985, with a collection of "little novels," *Saratoga, Hot,* and, in 1986, with *The Bobby-Soxer,* one of only two novels with a small-town setting. A year later she published *Age,* a spare, steely-eyed meditation on growing older. In 1988, she published a second nonfictional work, *Kissing Cousins*: on one level, an affectionate reminiscence of her kissing cousin, Katie Pyle, and on another, an exploration of her family's particular configurations of Southern, German, and Jewish backgrounds and ethos.

Many reviewers of Calisher's *Collected Stories* echoed the *Houston*

Chronicle reviewer's bewilderment—"Why some other fictionists are so well known and esteemed when Hortense Calisher is not has always been a mystery" and hoped that *Collected Stories* would earn Calisher the readership and acclaim she was due.[13] Calisher has, in fact, received a measure of recognition through the years. Her stories, four of which received O. Henry prize story awards, have been much anthologized. Two of her books, *False Entry* and *Herself,* were nominated for the National Book Award. In 1967 she received both a National Council of Arts Award and an American Academy of Arts and Letters Award. From 1986 to 1987, she served as President of American PEN and, from 1987 to 1989, of the American Academy and Institute. Since the 1950s, she has been a visiting professor at more than thirteen colleges and universities, including Barnard, Columbia, Stanford, and The University of Pennsylvania.

Many of Calisher's essays and reviews were reprinted in *Herself* (1972), an autobiographical work, but a characteristically idiosyncratic one: "Never a diary (she wrote other peoples'), partly a journal ... more than a memoir—for who wants to look back only?—she feeds it with fugitive soundings from a past she keeps up with" (*H,* 13–14). Essentially the autobiography of an intellectual and writer, the portrait that emerges is of a woman who shuns pigeonholing— of or by herself:

> My "mind"—as far as I can disinter it from the rest of me—seems to have no particular sex. I hold no special brief for "the family." I am greedy for experience, but more greedy for some than for others. What pulls me deepest, moves me darkly and lightly, is what I can think of as ordinary experience. *Sunt lacrimae rerum.* That's me. *Et mentem mortalia tangunt.* I find that line untranslatable, yet I am willing to spend my life at it: Here are tears for the affairs of men. They touch mortal minds; they touch mine. (*H,* 113–14)

There is nothing facile or readily accessible about the fictions that have resulted. And, not surprisingly, from early on in her career, style has been the shibboleth that has earned her both high praise and censure. All of Calisher's novels make demands upon the reader. A fast read through may very well lead to the conclusion that the style— sometimes, elliptical and compressed, othertimes, expansive and luxuriant—is, too often, unnecessarily difficult. Calisher, a consummate stylist, sometimes brings out the worst in her critics. In lieu of analysis, they often resort to ornate metaphors. In her review of *Textures of Life,* Maggie Rennert concludes that "Like a fine embroidered organdy, the texture is delicate and pleasing, the craftsmanship admirable. Life can be seen through it, but never clearly enough."[14] Others, apparently acting as the reader's watchdog, protest the demands exacted of the reader: "Calisher's [*False Entry*] will be much admired by the *cognoscente*. It carries forward the Jamesian tradition of rococo writing filigreed over hairsplitting thought."[15] Anthony Burgess faults her characters for being "too Calisherianly articulate."[16]

Still other reviewers of Calisher's *Collected Stories*—including such long time admirers as Anne Tyler, Doris Grumbach and Robert Phillips—prefer Calisher's short stories to her novels. It is not, writes Tyler, "that the novels are of lower quality, but to sustain this degree of intensity for any length of time is too exhausting for the reader."[17] Similarly, Doris Grumbach writes that "Prophetic revelation does not extend well."[18] Robert Phillips hopes that *Collected Stories* would "regain readers ... who have found it difficult to keep faith after experiencing her recent novels."[19] A common thread runs through these and other, far less favorable reviews: Calisher the novelist tends to stylistic excesses, indulging in technical virtuosity at the expense of plot and character.

Other reviewers, however, employ the vocabulary of some of Calisher's harshest critics—elliptical, supersubtle, Jamesian—in praise of her works. In his review of *False Entry*, Granville Hicks writes that "The style at least at first, seems rather mannered and indeed it is involved and allusive, but the further one goes the more one recognizes how beautifully it suits her purpose."[20] Surveying Calisher's work of the fifties and sixties, Robert Kiely writes that "Her fiction often reads like poetry, not merely because the language is charged with imagery, but because there is a concentration and intensity of expression which prohibits casual dialogue, comfortable description, mundane observations."[21] "[H]er most fervent readers," writes Marcelle Thiebaux, "will be those who savor the richly-imaged convolutions of thought and language."[22]

In his review of *The Bobby-Soxer*, Morris Dickstein pinpoints "the marriage of meaning and manner" (*H,* 42) so characteristic of Calisher's work:

> There are many writers who feel that the prose of a novel should be a transparent window on the world, that the novelist should never draw attention to himself or stand between his readers and his characters. I suspect Hortense Calisher never dreamed of being this kind of novelist. She belongs to a different tradition descending from Henry James, in which the writer's own complex intelligence—his humming eloquence, his subtle knowingness—becomes essential to his equipment as a storyteller. Far from holding the mirror up to life, this kind of writer diffracts it through the prism of his sensibility, as if to show how many-faceted it is.[23]

The prism of Calisher's sensibility is style, an ever-shifting angle of vision on a shifty reality, the ideal vehicle for her transportational theme. It is a fitting theme, indeed, for a writer who so long and resolutely has fled from absolutes and enclosures, a writer who, as she relates in *Herself,* has retained a keen hunger for more and varied experience:

Each stage of my life has seemed to me somehow an ascent, and a surprise—since here in my country one is supposed to decline toward the grave at an acute angle. . . . What has made this possible for me has been my peculiar "work" to which I have been as happily doomed. . . . There is a picture of me . . . at the age of nine or ten . . . holding the reins of a pony that is not my own. . . . I know that child's fortune. To be seized by work, and led through it to many loves. Perhaps the endpapers of this book . . . should pose that early picture against the later one the publisher will require of me, underneath the same invisible title: Waiting For More. (*H,* 397–98)

1

Bridging the Gulf: The Autobiographical Stories

Between 1948 and 1953 Calisher published eleven autobiographical stories; a twelfth appeared in 1965. In all but three of the stories, the protagonist is Hester Elkin and the narrator, her adult self looking back at crucial episodes in her youth. The stories are replete with details of a time long past (the earliest takes place during an Armistice parade in New York City), yet these are anything but exercises in nostalgia.

In his Introduction to the 1984 edition of *Collected Stories*, John Hollander argues that the autobiographical stories—grouped together here for the first time—interconnect but not in a "novelistic" way: "The continuity that does exist is provided more by an authorial sensibility and critical consciousness than by the family and the German-Jewish middle-class Manhattan of their milieu" (*CS*, xv).[1] However, beyond the unity created by the adult narrator's consciousness, there is, in fact, a novelistic unity. The theme of initiation clearly dominates each of the twelve stories: each culminates in a moment of epiphanic self-awareness. If the stories were to be rearranged in a biographically chronological order, that theme becomes at once more encompassing and more defined: a single (albeit, episodic) narrative takes shape, dramatizing Hester Elkin's rites of passage from childhood through adolescence to early adulthood.

The often uneasy triangle of parents and child looms large in these stories. By temperament and acculturation, Mr. Elkin is a turn-of-the-century Southern gentleman; the Austrian-born Mrs. Elkin, a twentieth-century dynamo. One is an easygoing and adoring father; the other is a demanding and hypercritical mother. The young Hester firmly allies herself with her father and his strategy for living; as the narrative progresses, however, what seemed once a neatly defined either-or reality becomes—given Hester's increasingly charged love-hate relationship with her mother—clouded and complex.

Hester's coming of age falls into distinctive stages corresponding to definite clusterings of stories. In the earliest stage, as seen in "Time, Gentlemen!" "May-ry," and "The Coreopsis Kid," the central relationship is between Hester and her father. But even as Hester basks in his uncritical love and warm, expansive nature, chinks in his armor appear. Although Mr. Elkin is only a peripheral figure at best in the second group of stories—"A Box of Ginger," "The Pool of Narcissus," and "The Watchers"—the essentially romantic approach to life he embodies is found to be woefully inadequate. Mrs. Elkin's brand of realism dominates the next group of stories, "The Gulf Between" and "Old Stock." Then, in two stories of emotional impasse—"The Sound of Waiting" and "The Rabbi's Daughter"—neither realism nor idealism seems to provide a strategy for living. Only in "Gargantua" and "The Middle Drawer" does Hester finally achieve a moment's delicate balance of two seemingly opposed sets of values.

The first group of stories introduces not only Hester's parents, mismatched in years and in temperament, but also Hester as the child between them—though not yet torn between them. The mood of "Time, Gentlemen!" is sweetly elegiac, as the narrator remembers, thirty years later, the daily ritual of getting Mr. Elkin off to work. Mrs. Elkin is only a peripherally disapproving, nagging presence, at war with her husband's "Victorian sense of time" (CS, 167). Like an English bartender calling "Time, gentlemen" at closing, she would clear her house of late-morning revelers. Mr. Elkin is described in loving detail:

> My father, born in 1862, and old enough to be my grandfather when I entered the world a year after his marriage to a woman twenty-two years younger than he, was by birth therefore a late Victorian. . . . [A] precocious, Alger-like energy—in his case combined with some of the bright, fairy-tale luck that comes to the third sons in Grimm—was to keep him all his life younger in appearance and temperament than others of his span. . . . (CS, 165)

Each workday morning sees a struggle between Hester's parents: "a parable in which Conscientious Practicality, my mother, strove to get Imaginative Indolence, my father, out of the house somewhere nearer to nine than noon" (CS, 168). That Mr. Elkin's business runs smoothly enough without him counts for little in Mrs. Elkin's mind; she craves "the appearance of frenzied toil" (CS, 167).

On this particular day (a quintessential one, really) young Hester is her father's ally and co-conspirator. His leisurely breakfast—calves' brains, first blanched, then sautéed—followed by meandering conversations with a succession of tradesmen, is matched by Hester's feigning illness so as to stay home from school. Both triumph: Mr. Elkin is still home at noon; Hester is home for the day. At the story's—and the day's—end, Mr. Elkin delights in the company of his family gathered around the dining room table: "We are all together with him in the now. . . . The lamps are lit for the night, against that death which is change" (*CS*, 175).

By situating that evening "in the now," a timeless present, the adult narrator still allies herself with her father. And yet, she also remembers, "with an Eurasian aching," her parents' "dividing voices" (*CS*, 172). They may be as different from each other as two continents, but the adult Hester now acknowledges what her childhood self could not: that she is native to both.

In "May-ry," Hester is once again the enthralled witness to a family drama which her father dominates. This time, however, she is not her father's ally: "he was the kindest man in the world, yet when the time came, it was my father who was purely unkind to our colored maid" (*CS*, 177).

Mrs. Elkin is again the censorious outsider, her disapproval this time directed at Mr. Elkin's easy, jocular relationship with their maid, Mary (pronounced "May-ry" by the Richmond-born Mr. Elkin). For ten years, the two have had an understanding: Mary's periodic drinking binges have been explained away as attacks of rheumatism. Although Mary is thirty-years old, Mr. Elkin considers her a child "and he loved all children. Just so long as she kept herself seemly in front of him . . . she was only doing what was expected of her" (*CS*, 179). So long as Mary drank outside the house and kept up her side of the long-standing fiction, Mr. Elkin was content. His home remained sacrosanct, protected from realities he would rather not face; hence, his adamant refusal to listen to Mary when, having decided to resign, she wants the truth finally out in the open:

> [He] positively refused to consider, to treat, to discuss, to *tolerate* a hint of what she wanted to tell him and he knew as well as she did. That she'd been lying all these years and wanted the dear privilege of saying so. (*CS*, 184)

Mary finally screams out the truth and leaves, never to return. Decidedly the Southern patriarch, Mr. Elkin is fiercely protective not only of his home but also of his long-held belief that blacks are essentially childlike.

"Time, Gentlemen!" and "May-ry," companion stories, dramatize what is at once one of Mr. Elkin's most and least admirable attributes: his determination to make his home a refuge. Her father's staunchest ally in "Time, Gentlemen!", Hester becomes his reluctant judge in "May-ry," and in so doing, takes a step back, however unconsciously, from her father's approach to life.

Mr. Elkin is again a dominant figure in "The Coreopsis Kid," a story which celebrates his unconditional love; for the first time, however, Mrs. Elkin is a presence to be reckoned with. Hester is a tall, ungainly nine-year-old, an only child who feels increasingly expendable and unlovable as her mother's second pregnancy comes to term. At a family garden party in the fall of 1918, Hester identifies herself with many of the party-goers, Mr. Elkin's eldely retainers, who "swam knowingly toward him out of the sea of incompetents" (CS, 187). Convinced, as only a nine-year-old can be, that the birth of a sibling will leave her, very literally, out in the cold, a banished waif, Hester especially identifies with Mr. Katz, the oldest and feeblest of her father's retainers: they two "were the worthless people, whom the practical people could not forever afford" (CS, 190). Her father was the magnanimous one, "[b]ut with Mrs. Elkin, some businesslike reason for being was expected" (CS, 190). The war's end and the baby's arrival signify the end of an era:

> the probable end of a halcyon time, after which expenses like herself and Katz, unless they could justify themselves in the meantime, might not be rescuable, even by her father, from her mother's measurement of worth. (CS, 191)

Hester becomes even more convinced of her own unlovableness when she compares herself to her female cousins: "a rosy wreath. . . . as closed to her as if they had locked hands against her, meanwhile interchanging the soft passwords of their pet names" (CS, 192). Seeing her face's reflection—"sallow, shuttered, and long"—she concludes that "It must lack some endearing lineament, against which people and language might cuddle. For it, a nickname was a status to be earned" (CS, 193).

The story ends with two celebrations, the Armistice Day parade and Hester's private rejoicing in the knowledge that neither love nor a nickname "was a status to be earned" (CS, 193). The discovery is a serendipitous one. Sent to collect Mr. Katz, whom Mr. Elkin has invited to the parade, Hester spots a photograph of her three-year-old self "in white corduroy bonnet with lining frilling her solemn face," inscribed by her father: "*Regards. From the Coreopsis Kid*" (CS, 199). Mr. Elkin, a manufacturer of fine soaps, talcums, and toilet water, including "Coreopsis of Japan" (CS, 199), had heralded the birth of "The Coreopsis Kid" with eight hundred telegrams. Here is the reassurance Hester has craved: she has always been lovable and worthy of a nickname in her father's eyes.

Still, the closing paragraph reveals how fragile and provisional Hester's personal armistice is. Like countless other well-wishers of the parading soldier, Hester holds an orange to throw. She is loathe to let go of this concrete symbol of her happiness:

> It was round, perfect, like the world at this moment. If there was a flaw in it, it could not yet be seen. She held onto it for as long as she could. Then, closing her eyes tight, she threw it. (CS, 203)

A world war may have ended, but Hester still sees the world as divided into warring camps; her familial dilemma persists: "there was no pleasing them—the practical ones. Yet they had to be pleased" (CS, 192).

As the narrative progresses, however, a more complex configuration evolves from the young child's unambiguously black-and-white view. In the next group of stories—"A Box of Ginger," "The Pool of Narcissus," and "The Watchers"—"the practical ones" prove to possess more interesting dimensions than the young Hester had imagined. And, just as the realists gain a certain ascendency, the romantics lose ground.

In "A Box of Ginger," Mr. Elkin is again the patriarch warding off painful truths. On the funeral day of his brother he cannot bring himself to tell his ninety-three-year-old mother of her son's death (having let her believe, through letters Mr. Elkin wrote in his brother's name, that her son was out West recuperating). Mrs. Elkin urges her husband to read the most recent "letter" to his almost totally blind mother, but it is Hester's nine-year-old brother, Kinny, feeling very adult and important, who volunteers for the task. His grandmother, quickly seeing through the sham, realizes that her son is dead. The story ends with grandmother and grandson embracing: "they rocked back and forth together, in a moment of complicity and love" (CS, 213).

Mr. Elkin's tender-hearted, essentially romantic approach to life is not denigrated (even his wife joins him in countenancing a comforting lie over a painful truth) but neither does it triumph, as in "Time, Gentlemen!" and "The Coreopsis Kid." And, in two other stories—"The Pool of Narcissus" and "The Watchers—the adolescent Hester becomes more acutely aware. In both stories Hester is still essentially an observer absorbing crucial lessons.

A tall, gawky twelve-year-old in "The Pool of Narcissus," ill at ease in her party dress of "lavender voile, its color harsh against her olive-brown hands" (CS, 218), Hester longs for the looks and bearing of Mrs. Braggiotti, the widowed mother of her friend, Clara, who "with her tilted nose, masses of true blond hair, and bud mouth, was just what every shag-haired girl staring into the Narcissus pools of adolescence hoped to see" (CS, 217). A moment's clear-sightedness threatens that romantic vision when Hester observes Mrs. Braggiotti

> wearing a pince-nez that mercilessly puckered the flesh between her brows, giving her the appearance of a doll that had been asked to cope with human problems. (CS, 217)

For a time, Hester manages to dispel any such unflattering and disquieting images of her idol.

Following Clara's birthday party, she and Hester accompany Mrs. Braggiotti and her unByronic suitor, George, to his soda fountain. There, Hester witnesses a brief but disturbing scene:

> Mrs. Braggiotti pushed George away sharply. "My shoe! Oh, you've got dirt all over my shoe!" She bent down to brush it, real distress on her face.
> "What is it you *do* want, Etta?"
> . . . "Why, I don't want anything, George," she said, in the same tone with which she had refused the sundae. (CS, 220)

Hester has heard enough to want out of "the dim island of the store . . . with its promise of suspension, of retreat" from the outside world (CS, 220). Her romantic idol unmasked as a paper doll with an emotional depth to match, Hester runs out into the cold, eager for "people she could jostle, buffet, and embrace" (CS, 220). In "The Coreopsis Kid," a younger Hester despaired of her long, sallow face, so painfully different from those of her conventionally pretty cousins. Here, she sees herself in a new, more flattering light: "Looking down at her hands, she thought suddenly that they were a good color; it was the lavender voile that was wrong" (CS, 220).

In "The Watchers," however, she learns to be wary of too much difference, of an unconventionality that leaves one too far out in the cold. Now fourteen years old, Hester has found another role model: her spinster aunt, Selena, who, like Mrs. Braggiotti, seems at first enviably detached from mundane concerns. Selena proves to be an even more chillingly cautionary figure, not because of anything she does, but, rather, because of Hester's closer identification with her.

Initially, Selena's aloof, Bohemian airs fascinate the silently rebellious teenager:

> Spare and dark-haired, the color of a dried fig, she wore odd off colors,
> like puce and mustard and reseda green. Although they did not become
> her, she carried them like an invidious commentary on the drab patterns
> around her, and her concave chest was heavily looped with the coral
> residue of some years' stay in Capri as an art student, in her youth. (CS,
> 223–24)

Hester envisions her aunt "living in the narrow, high rooms of one
of the single houses she associated with the very rich . . . from which
the humdrum truth of people would be inscrutably barred"—a house
all the more alluring since inimical to Hester's noisily busy "family of
Philistines" (CS, 224).

She is subsequently bewildered to discover that her idol is patheti-
cally eager for those Philistines' acceptance. Following Hester's grandmother's death, the Elkin household bustles with activity, and Selena,
her "cheeks . . . hennaed with an unaccustomed tinge of participation"
(CS, 227), performs the humble tasks assigned her. When, before
long, someone else takes over, Selena joins Hester on the sidelines.
What Hester admired and sought to emulate in Selena is losing its
romantic aura:

> For a long time the two of them sat there watching, while between them
> grew a tenuous thread of communion, as between two who sit at the
> edge of a party or a dance, sipping the moderate liqueur of observation,
> while around them swirl the tipsier ones, involved in a drunkenness the
> watchers do not share. (CS, 227)

Heard but not spoken in Hester's simile is the word, "wallflower."
At the story's close, Hester and Selena, her name unaccountably
missing from the list of family mourners, are left behind. Hester,

> In her mind, like a frieze . . . saw the added-up picture of Selena, always
> watching tentatively, thirstily, on the fringe of other people's happiness,
> and fear grew in her as she became suddenly aware of her own figure. . . .
> It was watching, too. (CS, 232)

More often than not, throughout the autobiographical stories, Hester's avidity for close, critical observation is cast in a far more positive
light.

The teenage Hester of the next two stories, "The Gulf Between"
and "Old Stock," is both observer and participant in familial and
social dramas that further complicate her view of adulthood. "The
Gulf Between" opens six months after the death of Mr. Elkin's
mother; his economic losses necessitate their moving from a spacious

apartment—Hester's home since birth—to another half its size. Mrs. Elkin's "village-sense of disaster," (*CS*, 234) for so long frustrated by affluence, rises or, depending on one's perspective, sinks to the occasion.

On this dismal moving day, "as always in time of crisis, her face had the triumphant look of disaster confirmed" (*CS*, 239). She makes the transition as unpleasant as possible, setting out dinner in cartons on the kitchen—rather than the dining room—table, as if to "forcibly show her family the ugly pattern of tomorrow" (*CS*, 240)—a pattern as much her design as one imposed upon them. When Mr. Elkin mildly protests the unnecessarily Spartan trappings, Mrs. Elkin responds with a cruel *non sequitur*, reminding her husband, twenty-two years her senior, that it is time the children realized their father isn't growing any younger. "[A]nxious as always to deny the ugly breach, to cover it over with the kindness that bled from him steadily" (*CS*, 241), Mr. Elkin turns his attention to Hester and her brother. An outraged Hester comes to her father's defense by taking the offensive. Hurtful *non sequiturs* are not solely her mother's domain: "'I wonder what I would have looked like,' she said in a hard voice, 'if you had not married her'" (*CS*, 242).

Later that night, Hester wakens to her parents' bitter quarreling. In much the same way that she fixed herself and Selena "like a frieze" at the conclusion of "The Watchers," so now she envisions her parents, frozen in place, poles apart:

On the one side stood her mother, the denying one, the unraveler of other people's facades, but resolute and forceful by her very lack of some dimension; on the other side stood her father, made weak by his awareness of others, carrying like a phylactery the burden of his kindliness. (*CS*, 244–45)

Hester's view of her parents' essential strengths and weaknesses suggests an impossible dilemma. What use to bridge the gulf between two so fundamentally flawed? Just as Hester's domestic world has shrunk to the confines of the small apartment, where, signficantly, the young Mrs. Elkin is now sole matriarch, so, too, has her perspective on the triangular relationship of parents and child. In the closing lines of the story, Hester, seeing herself "flawed with their difference . . . falling endlessly, soundlessly, in the gulf between. . . . began to weep the sparse, grudging tears of the grown" (*CS*, 245).

In "Old Stock," a story that occupies the same time frame as "The Gulf Between," Hester discovers other treacherous gulfs, but, disquietingly, ones all too easily bridged in the adult world.

The story opens with Hester and her mother on a train bound for the Catskills. The family's fortunes are still in decline, "but it would have been a confession of defeat for Mr. Elkin had he not been able to say during the week to casual business acquaintances, 'Family's up in the country. I go for weekends'" (*CS*, 264). Mrs. Elkin—blonde and beautiful, "whose blurred handsomeness bore no denomination other than the patent . . . one of 'lady'" (*CS*, 264)—is also intent on keeping up appearances. Today, however,

> there was that added look Hester also knew well, that prim display of extra restraint her mother always wore in the presence of other Jews whose grosser features, voices, manners offended her sense of gentility all the more out of her resentful fear that she might be identified with them. (*CS*, 263)

In contrast to her mother, all containment and silent censure, Hester, "feeling the rocking stir of the journey between her thighs," is exhilarated by "a verve of waiting" (*CS*, 263) for whatever life holds:

> nowadays it seemed to her that she was like someone forming a piece of crude statuary which had to be reshaped each day . . . that she was putting together from whatever clues people would let her have, the shifty, elusive character of the world. (*CS*, 264–65)

Soon after their arrival at the farm, Hester discovers that the world is shifty in ways she had not imagined. Mother and daughter escape the company of their fellow Jews to visit, as they have the two years before, the very Gentile Miss Onderdonk, an aging, laconic spinster and proud member of the "old stock," her dearest possession a "'Leather-Bound Onderdonk History'" (*CS*, 272).

The laconic spinster has dismissive words enough for the vacationing Jews and for Mrs. Elkin's informing her that she, too, is "Hebrew":

> "Never seen the Mister. The girl here has the look, maybe. But not you."
>
> *   *   *
>
> "Does you credit," said Miss Onderdonk. "Don't say it don't. Make your bed, lie on it. Don't have to pretend with me, though."
>
> *   *   *
>
> "Had your reasons, maybe." Miss Onderdonk tittered, high and henlike. "Ain't no Jew, though. Good blood shows, any day." (*CS*, 273)

Hester speaks out—"'We're in a book at home, too. . . . "The History of the Jews of Richmond, 1729–1917"'" (CS, 273)—but hers is a Pyrrhic victory. She has fought back, but on Miss Onderdonk's narrowly snobbish terms: "She had not said what she meant at all" (CS, 273). Later, upon returning to the farm, Hester is further confused by a radical realignment: the sight of her mother striking up a friendship with one of the formerly-scorned Jewish women from Manhattan, "one of the ones who said 'gorgeous'" (CS, 268).

At the story's end, it is dusk and "A thin, emery edge of autumn was in the air" (CS, 275)—fitting atmospheric conditions for the bleak, abrasive reality Hester now contemplates. About to enter the dining room, she steels herself for the "equivocal adult eyes":

> Something would rise from them all [the diners] like a warning odor, confusing and corrupt, and she knew now what it was. Miss Onderdonk sat at their table, too. Wherever any of them sat publicly at table, Miss Onderdonk sat at his side. Only, some of them set a place for her and some of them did not. (CS, 275)

The *New Yorker* publication of "Old Stock" precipitated a slew of censorious letters to the magazine and an angry newspaper article penned by a Cleveland rabbi. In *Herself* Calisher writes that her "sin was double":

> I had expressed some of these tormenting self-doubts which even the most outwardly impregnable Jew . . . may still be born with: Are "we" anything like "they" say we are? Are we defensively proud of being whatever we are because we have to be? . . . Would we really rather not be what we are? Worse, I had explored what must never be admitted to enemy forces—that there are divisions in our ranks. Not only divisions, but hierarchies. I had turned up the underside of our own snobberies. (57–58)

Like Hester, the young adult protagonists of "The Sound of Waiting" and "The Rabbi's Daughter" see only a series of numbing, inescapable compromises. Floundering in a world of closed doors, yearning for a "bright, fairy-tale luck" (CS, 165), Kinny (Hester's brother) and Eleanor (like Hester in all but name) despair of effecting a viable compromise between the romantic approach to life and an emphatically fact-bound one. At this stage, they are overwhelmed by the web of circumstance.

In the Introduction to her *Collected Stories*, Calisher describes Kinny and Eleanor as "youth revolving before the prospect of the world and not yet aware who they are" (CS, x). They are certain only of what they don't want out of life: Kinny despises his drudgery-ridden job as a welfare worker; Eleanor panics at the thought of joining the ranks of the many "shriveled, talented women" (*CS*, 287).

The twenty-one-year-old Kinny, recently graduated from college and living with his widowed father, is all too painfully attuned to "The Sound of Waiting." Working for the welfare department, now swamped with victims of the Depression, Kinny is tortured by "the driving sense of alienation, of constriction, that sent him out more and more on his free Saturday afternoons and Sundays" (*CS*, 251). Kinny is waiting for his life to happen, and the waiting is all the more difficult when he contrasts his with his father's youth.

In "Time, Gentlemen!" Mr. Elin's "fairy-tale luck" was merely alluded to; here, the saga of "the self-made American with the imprint of . . . the *bon vivant*, the *fin de siécle* beau-to-be" (*CS*, 248), is fleshed out. Kinny envies not his father's business successes but his amorous conquests: there was always, in Mr. Elkin's anecdotes, "an undercurrent that spread beneath his talk, moving provocatively under the lace of words like a musky perfume—the sense of beautiful women" (*CS*, 254).

"[L]istening to the echoes" of himself one Sunday afternoon, Kinny imagines waking his napping father—now in his seventies, his world shrunk to the confines of the apartment—to ask:

> "For what is it I wait?" Instantly the fantasy shrank, and he winced at the picture of the clumsy byplay that would really occur, knowing that between them lay the benumbing sleep of the years, a drowse from which it was not possible to wake. (*CS*, 257)

Instead, Kinny rushes out into the street, finding an illusory purposiveness in its activity. With no destination in mind, he nonetheless finds himself knocking at the door of one of his clients, a prostitute: "After the first compromise, he thought, all others follow" (*CS*, 262). The prostitute is a poor substitute, indeed, for those beautiful women of his father's youth.

A similar sense of constriction permeates "The Rabbi's Daughter." Eleanor is "a thin fair girl whom motherhood had hollowed, rather than enhanced" (*CS*, 276). A Juilliard-trained pianist with hopes of a professional career, she has become a weary housewife with neither time nor energy for practicing. Until her hawk-eyed aunt points out her work-coarsened hands—"'So . . . the "rabbi's daughter" is washing dishes!'" (*CS*, 280)—Eleanor has been blind to "the compromises that could arrive upon one unaware, not in the heroic renunciations, but erosive, gradual, in the slow chip-chipping of circumstance" (*CS*, 281).

Eleanor's dread of those compromises deepens when she arrives at a house that her engineer-husband has just rented in the Midwest. The "door-cluttered box" (*CS*, 285) is scarcely large enough for Eleanor's piano, which, in a moment of optimism, she had imagined practicing daily. Still in her travelling suit, as though loathe to admit she is "home," Eleanor plays a Beethoven andante and adagio—not, however, the scherzo movement. Her mood darkens considerably when she wonders: "will the denied half of me persist, venomously arranging for the ruin of the other?" (*CS*, 288) At the story's end, Eleanor breastfeeds her hungry infant: "'This one is still "the rabbi's daughter."' . . . At once it began to suck greedily, gazing back at her with the intent, agate eyes of satisfaction" (*CS*, 288).

Both "The Sound of Waiting" and "The Rabbi's Daughter" end on a somber note of capitulation; the two protagonists have arrived at the kind of impasse that the adolescent Hester had long feared would come about.

Two stories, "Gargantua" and "The Middle Drawer," stand apart from the rest, focusing as they do on Hester and her mother. The adult narrator recalls, with an admixture of love, anger, and gratitude, enduring lessons her mother taught her. Published in 1948, "The Middle Drawer" is Calisher's first autobiographical story, "Gargantua" (1967), the last; nonetheless, they are companion pieces.

The college-bound Hester of "Gargantua," still a gawky adolescent impatiently awaiting a miraculous sea change that will transform her into a beautiful, self-assured adult, craves confirmation of her potential from her mother:

> I wanted her to look at me squarely, not to tell me who I was . . . but to see me both for what I was and what I wasn't yet: a ragged creature but ready to be magnificent. . . . But that was the simpler part of it. . . . I thought I hated her, yet I wanted her to tell me how to be just like her. (*SH*, 7–8)

But her mother, in the hospital recuperating from an operation, sees (or at least, comments on) only Hester's clumsiness, laziness, and general ineptitude.

Hester, temporarily the woman of the household, enacts a nightly ritual. She finds herself inexplicably mimicking her mother, dining nightly on liver, the same dish—"plain, primal, a meat to be eaten without sauce" (*SH*, 9)—her mother, suffering from postoperation anemia, must eat. When Mrs. Elkin learns of this, she suddenly sees her daughter in a startlingly new light:

She was a woman of reserve . . . but this was one of the few times in our life together that I could be dizzyingly sure I had pleased. "You did it so that when I come home . . . so that you . . ." she said.

Wasn't this why I had done it, in part? Head bent, I nodded.

But in the matter of secrets, I was still in-between, no match for her. Her nose breathed in sharply. . . . "You're *rehearsing*!" she said.

. . . I saw that I had confused her, not as the chick can sometimes confuse an adult, but as the grown confuse the grown. She had lost her pure version of me. I was opaque. (*SH*, 12–13)

It is clear to the reader that Hester's act is a rehearsal on several levels. In a practical sense, Hester is preparing herself for the liver dinners she will soon cook for her mother. On another level, she is, perhaps, anticipating a time in the unforeseen future when she will be an invalid regaining strength; it is a rehearsal for some unhoped for contingency down the line. On yet another, deeper level, Hester is rehearsing for adulthood. Physically and temperamentally unlike her mother, she is imitating her in a small but concrete way. Mrs. Elkin, on the other hand, is eager that her daughter be like her in another way altogether: she wants Hester to become one of the sharp-eyed, sharp-eared realists.

Rarely light-hearted, Mrs. Elkin finds daily amusement in the bellowings of the gorilla, Gargantua, one of the attractions of the Madison Square Garden circus. She is especially amused to have to call Hester's attention to the low roars that Hester had taken for the city's anonymous sounds. She is more irritated than amused, however, when Hester mishears another, human bellowing, coming from the Irish woman in the next room. Hester hears "'Oh Lord. . . . Let not *my* will . . . but THINE . . . be done." Her mother's harsh "'*Listen!* . . . When are you ever going to start listening and looking at the world around you!'" focuses Hester's attention, and she hears: "'Oh Lord. . . . Let not *thy* will . . . but MINE . . . be done'" (*SH*, 17). At that moment, the adult narrator knows, "the satiric spirit . . . entered [her] life" (*SH*, 14).

A wonderful concatenation of events follows:

Three things then happened simultaneously. My mother and I burst out laughing—together. From the Garden, Gargantua began his morning calling. . . . And my father entered the room.

He didn't belong here, we felt that at once, not in the cozy nest we had all made for ourselves—the two of us, the unknown Irish girl, and Gargantua. (*SH*, 17)

That mother and daughter should "burst out laughing—together" marks a decisive and welcome truce in their strained relationship. As surprising, in light of all the other autobiographical stories, is their silently shared reaction to Mr. Elkin's presence.

There is yet another, sweeter surprise in store for Hester. Mrs. Elkin has caught a brief glimpse of Gargantua in her daughter's absence:

> "I guess I've been here too long. . . . But I swear to you, darling. It looked like nothing so much as an enormous old slice of liver."
>   So we'll never know, I said to her back then, what Gargantua really is. . . . And I didn't much care, for she had said "darling." (*SH*, 22)

The adult narrator remembers all of this when she is in the hospital recovering from a serious operation. At the story's close, Hester does not remember but instead imagines her mother's comforting words:

> "The beast that haunts us, the nameless," she says, "why it's nothing but an old slice of liver. Or while I say it is, in this merry-dark way whose lilt you hear yet—it *is* only that. There are things I can't decree away from you—such things, my darling. But while I say it is only that, I hold back the beast." (*SH*, 23)

Throughout the story, Mrs. Elkin tries to help her daughter in real and lasting ways by insisting she closely attend to the world about her. All her married life, Mrs. Elkin has felt that she has had to constantly watch over her husband, the family dreamer. She does not want her daughter to be, like him, in need of such vigilance. The adult Hester tries to pass the lesson on to her own children in "a certain old, dull meal" of liver she sometimes serves them: "'I'm the scourge, but *listen. Look about you in the world!*'" (*SH*, 23).

In an imaginative sense, Mrs. Elkin is her grown daughter's protector, just as Mr. Elkin had been the young child's, but there is a crucial difference: Mr. Elkin, the denier of ugly realities, did all he could to banish the beast from his home; Mrs. Elkin does not deny but transforms the "'beast that haunts us, the nameless'" into something harmlessly mundane, even ludicrous.

In "The Middle Drawer," the adult Hester momentarily "hold[s] back the beast" for her mother, a gesture that illustrates the great extent to which she has absorbed her parents' best qualities. The story opens a week after Mrs. Elkin's death. Having returned home to nurse her mother through her final months, Hester, key in hand, is on the verge of unlocking her mother's private drawer:

> There were no revelations to be be expected . . ., only the painful reitera-
> tion of her mother's personality and the power it had held over her own,
> which would rise—an emanation, a mist, that she herself had long since
> shredded away, parted, and escaped. (CS, 289)

What follows—Hester's bitter memories of past hurts—is ample
proof that she has not escaped and probably never will. As the story
unfolds, the reader discovers that the "reiteration of her mother's
personality" remains both a burden and a legacy.

"[M]otherless since birth and almost immediately stepmothered by
a woman who had been unloving, if not unkind" (CS 291), Mrs.
Elkin had grown to be a guarded woman, rarely capable of the "animal warmth" (CS, 292) the young Hester craved. Instead, between
them

> the barrier of her mother's dissatisfaction with her had risen impercepti-
> bly, like a coral cliff built inexorably from the slow accretion of carelessly
> ejaculated criticisms that had grown into solid being in the heavy fullness
> of time. (CS, 292–93)

One of the main sources of contention was Hester's passion for
reading:

> To her mother, marrying into a family whose bookish traditions she had
> never ceased trying to undermine with the sneer of the practical, it was
> as if the stigmata of that tradition, appearing upon the girl, had forever
> made them alien to one another. (CS, 295)

"One remote, terrible afternoon," Mrs. Elkin grabbed a book from
Hester and tore it in two. Filled with "the cold sense of triumph . . .
at the enormity of what her mother had done," Hester accused her
mother of thinking only of money; later, however, she realizes "that
her mother, too, was whipped and driven by some ungovernable
dream she could not express, which had left her, like the book, torn
in two" (CS, 295).

Hester's love-hate relationship with her mother continues into
adulthood: she wants both "to earn her mother's approval at the
expense of her own," and to "find the final barb . . . that would maim
her mother once and for all, as she felt herself to have been maimed"
(CS, 296). Hester has the chance when she returns home to nurse
her mother who is dying of breast cancer. She finds her mother

> moving unbowed toward the unspoken idea of her death, but with the
> signs on her face of a pitiful tension that went beyond the disease. . . . It

was clear she was suffering from a horror of what had been done to her and from a fear of the revulsion of others. It was clear to Hester, also, that her father and brother had such a revulsion and had not been wholly successful in concealing it. (*CS* 296)

When Mrs. Elkin asks Hester if she would like to see the mastectomy scar—an unmistakable plea for reassurance—Hester is engulfed by childhood memories of "the thousands of incidents when she had been the one to stand before her mother, vulnerable and bare, help-lessly awaiting the exactitude of her displeasure" (*CS,* 297).

In the next moment—the climactic moment of this story and, in-deed, of the cycle of autobiographical stories—Hester delivers not the long-anticipated "final barb" but the loving lie:

"Why . . . it's a beautiful job, Mother," she said, distilling the carefully natural tone of her voice. "Neat as can be. I had no idea . . . I thought it would be ugly." With a step toward her mother, she looked, as if casually, at the dreadful neatness of the cicatrix. . . . . (*CS,* 297)

Later, after her mother's death, Hester contemplates her mother's unwitting bequest: "fortitude. . . . But pity—that I found for myself" (*CS,* 297).

The stories written after this first autobiographical story declare otherwise, however; Hester has learned something about pity from her father. What she did achieve on her own was the successful dis-tillation of her parents' best qualities: steeliness and a keen, critical perspective from her mother; kind-heartedness and a sympathetic eye from her father. She has come to "read" the world the way Randall Jarrell advises one should read good poetry: "with an attitude that is a mixture of sharp intelligence and of willing emotional empathy, at once penetrating and generous."[2]

"The Middle Drawer" ends with Hester's recognition and accep-tance not only of her mother's legacy but also of "the innumerable small cicatrices imposed on us by our beginnings; we carry them with us always, and from these, from this agony, we are not absolved" (*CS,* 298). These words also mark the end of the autobiographical stories, as they appear in Calisher's *Collected Stories.* But the fitting close both to Hester's oftentimes stormy relationship with her mother and to the autobiographical stories as a whole appears in the conclud-ing paragraph of "Gargantua" (published twenty years after "The Middle Drawer"): "The people one lives with and loves can be like cornucopias in the mind; even after they are dead, we can abstract their riches, one by one" (*SH,* 23). Just as Hester has "abstracted the riches" of her parents, incorporating within herself their finest qualities, so Calisher, with a perspective at once piercing and embracing, has extracted the rich marrow of her early life, transforming it into stories at once powerfully evocative of a now distant past and startlingly contemporary in their sure, sensitive delineation of a young girl's rites of passage.

2

Coming Down from the Heights

Like many a beginning writer, Calisher drew first on her own life history, but, as she relates in *Herself,* "suddenly after less than a dozen close-to-autobiographical stories, their process is over; I want out, to the wider world" (*H,* 42). However wide the range of subjects in the stories, novellas and novels that followed this conscious change in direction, the rites of passage theme, with its climactic emphasis on moving outward and onward, persists. Hester Elkin of the autobiographical stories is the first of a succession of Calisher's protagonists to come out into a world in which change is the only constant.

Four of Calisher's novels, spanning her career and worlds apart stylistically, dramatize tumultuous transitions from adolescence to early adulthood. Central to all four is a movement—a recurring one in Calisher's fiction—from the heights of ingenious theorizing or emotional distancing to a grappling with problematic realities.

This movement is presented most straightforwardly, even schematically, in *Textures of Life* (1963), Calisher's second and most conventional novel. Its plot is a classically familiar one: young newlyweds, blithely confident they can live life on their own rarified terms, become gradually enmeshed in the convoluted, confining textures of everyday life.

The novel begins with the chilly wedding reception of Liz Jacobsen and David Pagani, nineteenth-year-old self-termed artists who barely conceal their disdain for this thoroughly tasteful, bourgeois occasion. Liz's antagonism has a more personal focus: her mother Margot, who "understood that her daughter's animosity toward her . . . was connected with her own very blameable dependence on nice things" (*TL,* 7).[1] Fearful of succumbing to a love of things, thus proving herself to be her mother's daughter, Liz's anger, "harbored like a gift, reassured her" (*TL,* 21).

So, too, does the newlyweds' new home, a fortress against the bourgeois. On their wedding night, Liz and David triumphantly survey their nearly empty New York City loft where "Space lay . . . like a weapon" (*TL,* 15) warding off middle-class trappings and values.

They are supremely confident that they can make of their life together "a significant arrangement—of the best" (*TL,* 29). That night ends, however, with another "significant arrangement": falling asleep with Liz in his arms, David,

> with all his family goods around him . . . looked like a man uneasily drowsing at his post but still sentinel against his Indians, his burden across his knees. He looked like a householder. (*TL,* 30)

As the novel proceeds, chronicling their first four years of marriage, they eventually acknowledge what the reader, thanks in large part to the narrator's gentle steering, suspects from the outset.

For a time, married life exceeds their expectations. Liz compares it to a tape measure, "all linear and good, back of that first black-marked inch a firm, satisfying nothing" (*TL,* 59). When their loft home proves less than ideal, and they move to another, larger loft, they welcome the chance to start anew. This move, however, triggers in Liz an obsessive and determinedly solitary home-making urge. Where space once lay like a weapon, things accumulate, "brooded over as if she were giving birth to her own fantasy" (*TL,* 108). Only her studio remains spartanly bare. The night of their housewarming party, the self-congratulatory metaphors of a "linear and good" life (*TL,* 106) no longer pertain. Their guests gone, Liz strikes a melodramatic pose: looping a rope around her neck she announces: "'housewife *and* interior decorator, hung by her own rooftree'" (*TL,* 113).

No longer can Liz and David congratulate themselves on being unanimous in all things. Liz's housewifely compulsions frighten her, while David feels that "marriage was daily clarifying his life and his work, leaving them free to be" (*TL,* 107). This particular night, however, mutual dismay reunites them when their widowed parents, Margot and Nicholas, telephone from California to announce their marriage.

On the surface, an unlikely pair—Margot is a stereotypically proper New York matron; Nicholas, a California artist who has led a quietly unconventional life—they forge a relationship that throughout the novel intermittently and ironically parallels the younger couple's, the older generation's tempered joy contrasting with their children's often boundless optimism.

When, some nine months later, Liz and David have a child, it again "seemed to both that they now had everything. They saw their way clear to seeing life clear" (*TL,* 170—until, that is, their infant daughter Mary suffers a series of convulsions. When Liz learns her daughter is severely asthmatic, another, darkly contrasting image supplants that of the unencumbered linear life; now she envisions

> the hook . . . a heavy mass that pushed up from below and protruded like a deformed sternum, around which the body reshaped itself like a grasshopper's tailcoat. (*TL*, 221)

At the novel's close, the generations seem, momentarily, to have exchanged places. The newly widowed Margot, invigorated by Nicholas's adventurous spirit, is traveling alone to Europe; Liz and David are heading for the California home Nicholas had built for himself and his son, Mary's asthma having necessitated their leaving a dust-filled loft.

Throughout the novel, Margot has anticipated, with an admixture of grief and anger, her daughter's eventual confrontation with unyielding realities. When it comes, however, she feels anything but righteous vindication:

> Still young in face. . . . [Liz and David] looked in some way exposed prematurely—as if, in whatever overnight experience had come upon them, only youth had kept their hair from turning white. (*TL*, 226)

Still, the novel ends on a guardedly optimistic note, with Liz's and David's realization that "It was not the end of things, only no longer the beginning" (*TL*, 248). Coming down from both literal and symbolic heights, they now see themselves as part of the "weave of life, that no one ever made" (*TL*, 248).

This change in perspective brings about artistic growth as well: by the novel's end Liz and David come to grasp how much they have yet to learn. Liz's early sculpted work is clearly self-obsessed: small waxen females, "all stylized toward the same anger" (*TL*, 194). Later, while pregnant, she sculpts a wooden torso of a neighbor's pregnancy-marked body, yet her subject is still essentially herself: scrutinizing the finished work, Liz "felt her own nakedness" (*TL*, 177). After Mary is born, she tries to capture the child in sketches and in clay figures, but "all kept to a stubborn abstraction" (*TL*, 175). These failures send Liz, newly humbled, back to art school, where she learns "of the power to be drawn from her own ignorance" (*TL*, 175). Later, grieving over her child's illness, Liz learns of the power to be drawn from suffering: she envisions not herself alone but also rows of figures suspended on the hook: not in wax, the malleable, fleshlike medium she has long preferred, but first in plaster, then in bronze— unmalleable, technically demanding, but enduring. Still angry, but no longer the adolescent who made a scapegoat of her mother, "she felt the angry balm, the upsurge of her powers—what it might mean to be an artist" (*TL*, 221).

Similarly, David's conditional sense of his artistic ability results from personal and artistic disappointments. Throughout most of the novel, he and a partner work on a film about people as seen solely through their objects. Considering David's intense pride in a life unencumbered by possessions, such a film could not help but be flawed by a condescending attitude. By the novel's end, David judges the completed film a failure: "the essential, overdocumented, had slipped the sieve" (*TL*, 245); what remains, surely, is a flashily empty technique. At this stage, his artistic dilemma, like Liz's, is paradigmatic—how to translate life into art:

> If one could imagine a loom, or looms innumerable, warp-and-woof radiating everywhere, perhaps not even from a center. The texture was so tight that one could never see, even over as much as four years of it, where any one part had begun. . . .
> But how in God's name would one show it pictorially? Or any way? It would be such an illumination of the obvious, stretched thin as a skin that enclosed all the world. (*TL*, 246–47)

Explicitly or implicitly, this question looms large in all of Calisher's longer fiction. The work itself is the answer—a provisional one, always, on the subject of what she describes as "our common unusualness."[2] Calisher recounts that "single story in all its variable" (*FE*, 229) in various styles. Of all of Calisher's novels, *Textures of Life* is the most conventional: even though the dialogue is characteristically elliptical and allusive, narration and description far outweigh it and, in a sense, fill in the gaps. Instead of a pervasive allusiveness, there is a mediating, controlling presence—the narrator's persona, mature and experienced, at some remove from her characters communicating directly with the reader.

In almost all of Calisher's novels and novellas, however, because they are so often cast in the form of memoirs, reports or journals, narrator and protagonist are one and the same. Regardless of plot, the drama of perception, of ways or styles of experiencing the world, dominates. Calisher's reviewers sometimes complain that the telling often obscures the tale. But given the fusion of narrator and protagonist, style—the self's hallmark—is necessarily foregrounded.

In none of Calisher's novels is that drama of perception so exuberantly celebrated as it is in *Queenie* (1973), her second novel of young adults' coming-of-age, which appeared eight years after *Textures of Life*. Like the young couple in that earlier novel, the protagonist of *Queenie* also comes down from the heights at the novel's close—in a double parachute with her lover. The style and tone of *Queenie* are a radical departure from the realistic, quietly modulated *Textures of Life* and, indeed, from Calisher's other novels. A comedy of manners and morals, set in New York during the Vietnam War period, the novel follows Alexandra Dauphine Raphael (Queenie, for short) from a happily unconventional adolescence to a happily conventional adulthood. Her literal descent, as comic and unexpected as everything that has preceded it, is the objective correlative of a willingness to enter into the weave of everyday life.

Queenie recounts her coming-of-age in a series of questioning monologues: for two-thirds of the novel she directs these "cloud confessions" at august representatives of university, state, and church—God included. The novel is a contemporary *Pamela:* like Richardson's heroine, Queenie assiduously records her thoughts and experiences—but on a tape recorder. And, unlike her long-suffering predecessor, this twentieth century New Yorker intends to lose her virginity with all due speed.

From the outset, it is clear that Queenie is no typical sixteen-year-old beset by predictable angsts: "A happy childhood can't be cured. Mine'll hang around my neck like a rainbow, that's all, instead of a noose" (*Q*, 13). Queenie's upbringing has been enviably secure, loving, and, by bourgeois standards, shocking: she "was born and raised to be a kept woman" (*Q*, 14) by Aurine, an old-fashioned courtesan, who is either Queenie's aunt or her mother, and by Oscar, Aurine's lover and perhaps Queenie's father.

Queenie, an old-fashioned girl in a modern world, has had an atypical education—"I didn't hear about the mysteries of life, I got the recipes" (*Q*, 37)—but she suspects they may prove unusable beyond her family's charmed circle. In the novel's opening section, Queenie's ostensible confidante is a college admissions director to whom she is addressing the standard self-descriptive essay. In this never-to-be-mailed letter, Queenie wonders if she, like her role model, Aurine, can "be happy and successful these days without penis envy?" (*Q*, 68). To her surprise, she does not have to wait for college for the answers. They come, tuition-free, in the course of three parties, at once Queenie's farewell to childhood and her debut as a sexual, albeit still virginal, creature.

The party scenes are wonderfully executed set pieces, each a miniature comedy of manners in which the male ego and, sometimes, male organ come under scrutiny. In this section, "A Heart Without Envy,"

Queenie's imagined mentor is a priest—not such a curious choice, given Queenie's growing determination to situate the sexual in the theological.

The first of Queenie's farewell/coming-out parties, which Oscar hosts for his cronies, is a sedate affair. Dressed demurely, as though to help her aging admirers forget time's passing, Queenie is a keenly observant guest of honor, eager to fathom men's mysteries. At the party's climax—Aurine's highly theatrical entrance—Queenie suddenly sees Oscar's friends in a radically different perspective:

> I can see what *they're* envying. They don't envy us, of course, her or me. . . . Can it be they're all envying their former, other, better days? Can it be a man spends most of his life envying *himself*? (*Q*, 88)

A provisional answer materializes after the second party—this one hosted by Aurine at her restaurant for her courtesan friends—where, once again, the male ego intrigues and baffles Queenie. The ancient maitre d', Marcel, his dignity inexplicably marred by a continuous smirk, serves course after course of "strange, dark food" (*Q*, 100). This party climaxes with his drunken revelation: avenging a blow to his ego—Aurine's hiring a new chef, also named Marcel—he has flavored the several courses with his own wine-fortified urine. Again, the uniform expression of pride on men's faces puzzles Calisher's heroine; more astounding, however, is Oscar's gleeful response to her exclamation that a woman would never consider such a reprisal: "'Queenie—it's even truer a woman couldn't'" (*Q*, 106)—certainly, given the circumstances, not with such facility.

Queenie concludes that there may, then, be a cause for penis envy since it is clear now that a penis can defeat the most subtle woman. Ruminating on the theological implications of the evening—"Is God really as queer for men as they are?" (*Q*, 115)—Queenie glumly contemplates a God-ordained male superiority.

Following the climax—or, literally, the anti-climax—of the third and final party, a "family" affair at the home of one of Aurine's fellow courtesans, Queenie thoroughly revises her "penis theology." The women's collective erotic aura so intoxicates Queenie's musically-named date, Schubert Fish, that he lies in wait for her in a darkened room. For a moment, Queenie seriously considers losing her virginity, until Schubert's "five little prideful words"—"'And it's not circumcised either!'" (*Q*, 146)—precipitate explosive giggles from Aurine and friends, hiding, ever-watchful of their ward. The result is "the kind of fall you have to stand up and button your fly over" (*Q*, 147).

Following this third lesson in male pride—and in its downfall—
Queenie not only feels a shade less virginal; she also happily concludes
that penis envy is a myth designed to protect its vulnerable idol. She
now knows why Aurine has a heart without penis envy: "People who
have the power plant don't need to have power complexes"; the distaff
counterpart of penis theology now holds sway. Men have the envy;
women, the heart; and "God is for cunt" (*Q*, 152).

On this triumphant note, Queenie's childhood—and the first section—end. Confident about what she has, if not what to do with it,
she enters college, "the Hencoop," where along with the other "eggs
in an incubator," she is "Chicked!" (*Q*, 155).

In this section's monologue—Queenie's term paper on herself—the
time for action has arrived: "no thoughts are any good unless you *lay
your bod on the line* with them" (*Q*, 156). What better way to affirm
these two new convictions than actively to research what old-fashioned parlance termed an orgy: the "fuck-in" (*Q*, 181). Faced with a
dizzying number of politically correct orgies, Queenie chooses a
"'grieve-in'" (*Q*, 187), a ballroom full of people "rocking together
for social action" (*Q*, 204), protesting everything from "'Poison
nerve gas!'" to "THE DATING SYSTEM IN SCHENECTADY"
(*Q*, 204). Any doubts Queenie has had about being an old-fashioned
girl soon disappear: she is "stuck with this sneaking perversion for a
twosome" (*Q*, 207) and by the conviction that "*Doing it for no reason
must be best*" (*Q*, 215).

Priorities now in order, Queenie leaves college. Dowry packed (her
taped monologues, a $50,000 diamond and a *cache-nombril* in which
to display it), she, happily and without much preamble, loses her
virginity to Giorgio, a friend since childhood. Although Queenie is
still the nonstop monologist, she no longer needs "interlocutors":
"People to report to, imaginary or otherwise. Life enhancers! Father
images who can't talk back" (*Q*, 223). With Giorgio, more often in
than out of bed, she realizes that "Doing something means you don't
have to describe it" (*Q*, 235). Even so, Queenie, true to form, continues to record everything but the sex act.

The real and surreal merge in the novel's concluding section. Giorgio's latest vocation—hijacker "Of anything anywhere" (*Q*, 243)—
culminates in a grand and grandly fantasized coup: hijacking the
president of the United States (clearly Nixon, though unnamed).
Queenie and Giorgio exit the plane, which may or may not contain
the hijacked president, in a double parachute. The girl raised in a
"sky-village" (*Q*, 17) on "Fifty-Seventh-Street-and-penthouse-Sev-
enth Avenue" (*Q*, 13) finally touches ground: she and Giorgio, "hap-

pily stuck with each other, in a realistic way" (*Q*, 273), contemplate marriage: "'Call it the call of the wild,'" says Giorgio. "'Toward the conventional'" (*Q*, 275).

In *Queenie*, Calisher embellishes an adolescent's coming-of-age with the comic, the farcical, even the fantastical: the coming-out parties, the political group grope, the jet-hopping revolutionary's life. Correspondingly, she has created a style (embodied in the persona—or, more accurately, the voice—of Queenie) that weaves a richly comic web around typical adolescent questions: Who am I and what do I want?

The novel's exuberantly ornate style—inseparable from Queenie's voice—is contemporary baroque; indeed, the novel itself is a modern-day version of an eighteenth century *opéra bouffe*. Calisher introduces the analogy toward the novel's close when Giorgio, having listened for the first time to Queenie's taped monologues, describes her life as "a cross between light opera . . . and broad *opéra bouffe*" (*Q*, 245). Indeed, like a typical *opéra bouffe*, the novel is

> rapid in movements, having much repetition of short motifs, a disjunct melody line, comic effects produced by sudden offbeat accents, . . . and an infectious gaiety and vigor of utterance.[3]

In this contemporary version, Queenie is both heroine and performer (a musical correspondence to her dual role as narrator and character); like a well-trained *bel canto* singer, she is adept at both improvisation and ornamentation. Her skill at both is put to the test in the novel's concluding pages since Giorgio, inspired by Queenie's tapes, has decided to become a theatrical impresario. He envisions a New York musical of her life: "*Queenie—An Old-Fashioned Girl*" (*Q*, 219). Eager for even more material, he urges Queenie on. Trooper that she is, she improvises such highly ornamented arias and recitatives as

"Female Confessing. Recitative":

So, no more La Pasionaria for me? Tha-ats pop!
But secretly . . . after the first half-hour of social
      justice, ain't it all shop? . . .
uh dress the *wound*, uh give the *blood*, uh lead
      the *blind* . . . and   then   Stop?

. . . Maybe after the first half-hour *everything*
      is pop—
andlovebetweenthelegs isonlypossible because it
      needn't take that long?

—Or between any places you choose, of course.
. . . So here's my song:
(*seriously*)
Ah tigerbaby of life, sucking your milk, seeking
   your vineshade, I know you! It's me!
Getting laid. And I just want to be. I just want to be.

(*naturally*)
and who cares if I overslept?
I'm being *kept*. (*Q*, 268)

Queenie's ebullient songs paradoxically celebrate her coming down to earth, putting "one prosy foot after another" (*Q*, 267) in rhyme. Despite her nickname, she is neither a regal figure safely above the fray, nor a contemporary La Pasionaria, the Spanish Communist famed for her fiery oratory. Still, Queenie relishes her distinctive voice, her distinctive angle of vision. In an aphorism that would be equally at home in Calisher's autobiography, Queenie declares: "'I don't mind being a feminist on my own. Once you join the others, you're a unionist'" (*Q*, 267).

Queenie concludes, as do all of Calisher's novels, not at the end but at the beginning of a journey— this one both literal and metaphorical—with a comically ambiguous *envoi*: "'Ciao, childhood. . . . Be happy.' I don't know yet whether I mean hello or goodbye." The "ciao," Queenie realizes, is aptly chosen: "What else can you say when you are traveling?" (*Q*, 282). Wherever her travels lead, it is certain that her happy childhood will be a legacy in and a talisman against a fashionably graceless world. For beneath the novel's broad jokes, the satiric stabs at sixties' radical chic, lies a norm befitting the novel's comic universe: the family as love nest and haven, where a general benevolence reigns. Queenie's coming of age is, in a sense, both a coming back to and a departure from that norm.

Two years after *Queenie*, Calisher once again wrote of a young New Yorker's coming of age during the Vietnam era. The fictional universe of *Eagle Eye* (1973), however, is anything but comic. Like Queenie, Quentin "Bunty" Bronstein grows up in a comfortably middle-class household, the only child of doting parents, though theirs is no happy love nest. The twenty-two-year-old Bunty sums up that mutedly unhappy triangle:

There was a terrible fragility about the Bronsteins. That they didn't know of. Their kid did his best to act accordingly. In all the Boy's Lives of famous men he had ever read, there was this simple beginning, in which the boy was held transparent in the vial of family, to grow. While the life put one foot after another, scattering little grenades of bread that even in the city would one day lead out of the forest, in single file.

They all three thought they were leading a linear life. (*EE*, 14)

Just as Queenie's exuberant voice generates a distinctive world, in which a happy ending is assured, so, correspondingly, does Bunty's densely convoluted consciousness establish the darker tenor of *Eagle Eye*. Although Bunty's voice dominates, it does so, for the most part, in the third person: clearly, a tactic to objectify himself in the face of his overwhelming subjectivity, to get a bead on his own life.

Bunty is the titular Eagle Eye who, the morning after his twenty-first birthday party—"A year late, but it should last a lifetime" —knows he must begin "sweating out the world" (*EE*, 10). The party, with its disquieting revelations about his parents' disintegrating marriage, brings to an end Bunty's attenuated adolescence. After a series of flashbacks to his youth and to the previous year's travels abroad, the body of the novel focuses on the evening of the party and on Bunty's efforts, in the months following, to widen his vision, to make sense of his life, past and present, individual and familial. It is not enough, he discovers, merely to retreat from his parents' world. He must see through and beyond their attempts to "dwarf the world" (*EE*, 227) to a speciously manageable reality, if he is to home in on what makes his life worth living, on "what's worth murdering for" (*EE*, 10).

Looking back at his childhood, Bunty recalls material gains and psychic losses. His parents, Buddy Bronstein, a self-made business-man, and Maeve, once Buddy's secretary, are upwardly mobile in the extreme, moving from a good address to a better one, jettisoning people and possessions along the way. Their relentless acquisitiveness "diminsh[es]" (*EE*, 17) Bunty, who silently rebels against their "linear life." Craving permanence, he wants to be "where his future was indissoluble from his past, friends passing and repassing in a guild he knew" (*EE*, 13). From childhood on, Bunty retreats, eagle eyed, to an interior eyrie, safely distant from his parents' undefined but joint "energetic sadness" (*EE*, 23).

After a year abroad, spent not dodging but avoiding being drafted into the Vietnam War Bunty returns to the familial battleground, to the most grandiose apartment—"oh, so we're richer, we're that kind of rich now" (*EE*, 67)—and to disconcerting changes in his parents: theirs is no longer a joint sadness. Maeve, though looking younger, more beautiful, seems ghostlike, curiously detached not only from her husband and guests but also from the son she once doted on. She communicates with him to warn him about his father:

"Buddy's afraid to be rich. He has to have somebody to lay it on. But the peacock has to stand very still. Take his money, if you have to. I earned it. But get away somewhere." (*EE*, 155)

At this anything but festive occasion, Bunty feels a stranger among other—mostly hostile—strangers, observing the guests as if separated from them by a great chasm: youth on one side; age, shabby with compromise, on the other. He connects only with a young woman, a homeless transient, who has crashed the party. Otherwise, his encounters with the middle-aged guests—notably, with Janacek, a famed child psychiatrist, and with a Catholic priest, Father Melchior—are sparring matches with would-be father figures who seem bent on converting him to their particular system of "world dwarfing."

Bunty soon discovers that Maeve herself is intent on escape. Like Liz and David in their loft, Queenie, with her penthouse "cloud-confessions," and Bunty himself in his interior eyrie, Maeve, too, has taken to the heights—her intent, however, is to fall. She retreats from others, especially her husband, in the penthouse's terrarium: "a bulb of opaline glass . . . extruded on air again, as if the building had blown a last bubble before it gave up its climb" (*EE*, 85). Sensing some danger connected with it—even the plants seem to want out—Bunty discovers that she has made it her private death trap, filling the pots with ball bearings that have weighted the terrarium past its safe limitations. Bunty escapes the terrarium just before it begins to fall, Maeve leaves with the psychiatrist, and Buddy takes his son to the one place where he is most at home, his penthouse office.

Later, following a guided tour of his father's "lair" (*EE*, 174)—the equivalent to Maeve's terrarium—with its bird's-eye view of Manhattan, Bunty is caught off guard: his father's world-dwarfing encompasses the past as well as the present. He has filled one of the rooms with *his* father's office furnishings and with the "worn possessions which drop off a family as it jogs, never to be seen again" (*EE*, 179). The room is Buddy's attempt to save the past, but it is windowless, dustless, mothless.

Bunty wants not only "to live in a room that is real" (*EE*, 185) but also to save what is real and hopes that his father's computer, an IBM 7090, may hold the key: "'Oh God. . . . Oh God god. . . . The Lord is my shepherd. Here you are'" (*EE*, 177). Bunty once had a passing teenage infatuation with the same model, nicknamed "Batface." The urge to deify the computer quickly comes and goes: "Old Batface will do exactly what you tell it to—right or wrong. As all the manuals assure us, it is the perfect fool." Even so, he takes heart from knowing that the computer—unlike his parents—"can't lie, like a man does.

To itself" (*EE,* 136). Soon after, Bunty wonders if the computer might hold the key to processing his memory and, by extension, his life:

> if one day you fed it all the clues of meditation that you had with you, the little blurts and jargons that kept you going but hidden, and meant you to yourself like you own vibration in the dark. . . . (*EE,* 12)

Hoping to build, and, thus, possess permanence, Bunty once planned to become an architect. He has now found another vocation, one mixing memory, desire—and design:

> It's no trick at all to break away from a family. . . . You can cut up a family in one day's night. With the facts. . . . But where do the facts go then? Can they be saved? Maybe there's a vocation in that. (*EE,* 185)

Unlike his parents, Bunty wants to meld present and past. The computer may prove, he hopes, to be his state of the arts' *deus ex machina.* After months of weekend sessions with "Batface," Bunty outlines his ambitious project to his father:

> "A consultation service; organizing a man's knowledge of his own life. . . . It would be a life-bank like the records the government is building. Only every man for himself." (*EE,* 197–98)

Before Bunty's proceeding with his plan, however, he needs to put his still nascent adult self to the test. The night of his party, Bunty had warded off various proselytizers: his father, the psychiatrist, and the priest. Now he seeks them out, eager to try to answer, essentially, the very questions Queenie put to herself: "What's smart about me? What's dumb?" (*EE,* 185).

In these three charged encounters—somber parallels to Queenie's three coming-out parties—the notion of audience, briefly alluded to earlier in the novel, takes on an emotional urgency. As a child, Bunty was painfully conscious that his parents' scenario of their family life needed an audience—himself—to confirm it. Buddy played the part of the affable, self-effacing tycoon; Maeve, "inside the shell she made to be looked at" (*EE,* 87), played the movie star; and Bunty was their "Bunty-doll" (*EE,* 186), "a kind of mule-stupid dollbaby he scarcely recognized" (*EE,* 32). Unlike Queenie, he seeks out real rather than imaginary father figures or audiences.

He refuses to play the role of "Bunty-doll" with the psychologist Janacek, who, like Bunty's parents, is dangerously hungry for control and for an audience. Theirs is a sparring match: Janacek wants infor-

mation only Bunty can provide about Maeve, now under the doctor's
wing; similarly, Bunty wants information from Janacek about a dead
woman named Jasmin, who had been Janacek's estranged wife and,
for a brief while, Bunty's lover. Their basic antagonism stems from
Janacek's refusal to confront painful, guilt-saturated memories—beginning with early years in a concentration camp as the son of a camp
guard—and from Bunty's determination to remember and thereby
save his past, including those, like Jasmin, lost to death. Their conversation ends in a stalemate: "We've done our bit for each other, that's
all. But I'm not his style of listener" (*EE*, 192).

Much to Bunty's surprise, he is Father Melchior's style of listener.
Initially, however, Bunty's defensiveness—he is wearing mirror sunglasses—prevents his seeing the man before him: humble, kindly, and,
like Bunty himself, a man struggling to come down from the heights.
The priest, soon to leave the priesthood for married life, does not
want to convert Bunty. As Father Melchior sips his wine and Bunty
smokes his joint, they come to be "like cronies" (*EE*, 216). In parting,
Bunty presents the priest with one of his prized possessions, a knife
with thirty-nine uses: "'A wedding gift. Keep it for the road'" (*EE*,
216). It is a quietly significant moment in Bunty's life. Previously, he
had wanted to keep fast both people and possessions. Now, in response to the priest's question—"'Can you spare it?'"—Bunty answers: "'I'll remember I had it once. And that it wasn't lost'" (*EE*,
216). As a child, Bunty watched helplessly as people and things
slipped out of his life; later, his emotional possessiveness would be a
match for his parents' materialism; now, finally, he freely relinquishes
what once he would have clung to.

Bunty's visit with his father is framed by the other two, thus em-
phasizing the polarities of the father-son relationship: on the one
hand, there exists between them the kind of tension and suspicion
that characterizes Bunty's meeting with Janacek; on the other, there
is the hoped for but never realized acceptance and unspoken rapport
that he and Father Melchior enjoy.

Bunty's meeting with his father is especially painful, and important,
because it will be their last. Buddy, dying of kidney failure, is in the
hospital, the last of his controlled, sterile environments: both physically and emotionally, he is unable to rid his system of wastes. Wearing
mirror sunglasses once again, Bunty has shielded himself for the occasion: clearly a tactical move to both maintain a safe distance and to
weaken the performer-audience relationship between himself and his
father. When, however, Buddy exchanges his glasses for Bunty's, a
moment's truce occurs: "In the mirror-lenses, I saw myself, in him"
(*EE*, 199). As in the climactic moment in "The Middle Drawer" when

Hester examined her mother's scar and "they stood eye to eye for an immeasurable second, on equal ground at last" (*CS,* 197).

This genuine, albeit silent, rapport is, however, short-lived. Bunty tries to buoy up his dying, despairing father—"'Take it easy. . . . You were brought up to expect the best. . . . Us to expect the worst. It'll work out'"; his father counters with an automatic, patronizing response Bunty remembers all too well: "'Smart. . . . Very smart'" (*EE,* 199). Once alone, Bunty weeps for them both: "My tears for him sluiced through my fingers like his money. Nothing I could do for him either way. Live an imitation life, you get an imitation death" (*EE,* 200).

At the novel's close, Bunty is about to leave, Batface in tow, for a Berkeley think tank, where he hopes to create "A computer-dating-process with your own mind" (*EE,* 224). But first, he, like the protagonists of *Textures of Life* and *Queenie,* comes down to earth: a mugger's blow to the head leaves him "down in the gutter, dirty, and not ashamed of it." Mirror sunglasses gone, "His vision was 20-20 now. . . . He was Batface, had been all along. Bunty to Quentin, Batface to Eagle Eye, one plane ticket would carry them all" (*EE,* 245).

Although Bunty's father has died and his mother and Janacek "are revisiting the death camps, one by one—A pilgrimage, to dwarf the world" (*EE,* 223) into one suffering entity—Bunty is not alone: "The Bronsteins were moving again; it was his heritage. Though it was the ports that bothered him, he would settle for the journeys" (*EE,* 248). Like the protagonists of *Textures of Life* and *Queenie,* Bunty is on the verge of a Janus-faced journey: he is saying both hello and goodbye to his past. More important, he has finally come to embrace the journeying life. Suffering and loss have generated for him, as for Liz in *Textures of Life,* a new metaphor for his life:

> The jangle of personality that everybody was, rode along with him, a tinkle of manacle at the wrist, a chain gang at the anklebone. The song of the first loss, training him. What are we here for, here for, if not to see each other's lines of force? And see them, see them pitiful? (*EE,* 248)

Bunty's basic dilemma, that of a young man grappling with family, loss, and his own still provisional identity, may be commonplace, but the novel's style—allusive, elliptical, poetically compressed—makes an old story new. Many reviewers, criticizing the novel for the absence of a straightforward, easily accessible narrative, failed to see that the novel's style is necessarily inseparable from its meaning. *The New Yorker*'s anonymous reviewer complained specifically against "the con-

stant intrusion of phrases like . . . 'his father's linear reality'"—one of
the novel's most significant phrases (and one that creates a strong
metaphorical link with *Textures of Life*).[4] Stylistically as well as thematically, the novel opposes "the linear life" of facile explanations, of
formulaic responses. At the novel's end, Bunty undergoes a radical
reorientation. Embracing "Process [as] the reality" (*EE,* 202), he
gives up on the quixotic idea of exhaustively recording his life and
begins improvising at the computer keyboard—a high tech parallel
to Queenie's impromptu arias that also celebrate how "[T]heory keeps
us up, flesh sends us down" (*Q,* 206) from interior eyries.

Improvising life and art also constitutes the thematic center of *The
Bobby-Soxer* (1986), published thirteen years after *Eagle Eye*. The unnamed narrator/protagonist recalls a formative three-year period in
her youth when she, too, puzzled over the intricate weave of familial
relationships and the hazy contours of her still nascent adult self. Now
a successful, middle-aged actress, she conjures up that teenage self—
a 1950s bobby-soxer—who, impatient for "gestures of [her] own"
(*B-S,* 90), assiduously studied the gestures of others, living and dead.
As in the autobiographical stories, the adult consciousness plays a
peripheral role, allowing the younger self to come center stage.

In this, one of two Calisher novels to be set in a small town—"we
lived on one of those streets [the narrator relates] where the existence
of, well, real life, could not hope to be concealed" (*B-S,* 3)—the
protagonist discovers that "real life" can indeed remain concealed,
despite dogged efforts to bring it to light. At the heart of the novel
lies a remembered collaboration to plumb a family mystery between
the teenager, who dreams of acting, and the middle-aged Craig Towle.
A native son, now famous playwright, Towle has long been fascinated
by a woman he never knew, the protagonist's great-aunt Mary Leona,
known as Leo, who was rumored to be physiologically both male and
female. Returning to research a play about her, Towle enlists the aid
of the the young girl (who bears an uncanny facial resemblance to
Leo) in an imaginative recreation of Leo's elusive personality and
secluded life.

The project appeals to the teenager for various and complicated—
even contraditory—reasons. Craig Towle, "the dark man of all this
town's sonnets" (*B-S,* 47) strongly attracts her both sexually and intellectually. Earlier, she has compared herself "quite pleasantly [to] the
six-foot Trilby in the old illustrated DuMaurier" (*B-S,* 41). Although
Towle is no latter-day Svengali transforming a young model into a
renowned singer, he does help mold a young girl, a sometime model
for her sculptor boyfriend—into an actress.

She wants to recreate Leo for still other motives that safeguard her

autonomy and make the project her own, even as they further implicate her into the familial weave. Aunt Leo is a family mystery she
feels she has inherited; her gravitation toward family—in her case,
three living generations—is a constant in the novel. Like Bunty Bronstein in *Eagle Eye* who knew that "It's no trick at all to break away
from a family" (*EE*, 185), she resolves to save, not sever, those bonds:
"I never dreamed of disowning either my family or the town, whether
or not I left them. I meant instead to grasp them for all they were—
if I could find that out" (*B-S*, 74).

Of all the families in Calisher's works, this is the most labyrinthine
in its emotional and sexual configurations: a communal counterpart
to Leo's sexual inclusiveness. The protagonist's bisexual father has a
lover—not, as she assumed, a kept woman in New York but a wealthy
man—who bequeathes a considerable fortune to the protagonist and
her younger brother, Tim. Her mother also has a love affair—with
Craig Towle. By the narrative's end, Tim, a practicing homosexual in
his youth and early adulthood, is about to marry and their parents,
now in South America, have embraced celibacy—he in a monastery
and she in a nunnery.

Midway through the novel, this atypical nuclear family expands to
include five men—the protagonist's father and brother, a Japanese
servant, her father's South American business associate and probable
lover, her own lover, Bill; and four women—grandmother, mother,
and daughter, and the Japanese servant's wife. The protagonist calmly
concludes that "It is awesome, to confront all the divisions at once.
Yet who can regret knowledge?" (*B-S*, 139).

"[A] shell waiting to be filled with meaning" (*B-S*, 157), she, like
the protagonists of the other novels of young adults' coming of age,
is bent on finding a vocation. Initially, she aspires to be a painter but,
like the protagonists of *Textures of Life*, is caught up short by her
inability to capture on canvas the impossible—her life's essence: "all
its underlayers were perfectly clear to everybody—and my brush had
not known how to make this evident" (*B-S*, 4). Still, she determines
to find some way of translating consciousness into act: "However I
was to perform it—if not in paint or words, then perhaps by sacrific-
ing bits of my own flesh . . . this observing was the adventure I was
fitted for" (*B-S*, 46). Not only observing, but being observed, she is
eager to recreate Leo who will then be "seen *being*" (*B-S*, 202).

Two other women in the novel shrink from being seen, however. Just
as the protagonist sees Leo as her mysteriously elusive double, so, also,
does she identify strongly with these other elusive personalities: her
mother and the novel's other bobby-soxer, Towle's young wife. All
three are under Towle's spell; sexually, all move "questward" (*B-S*, 57)

toward him, but two fall by the wayside. Towle's wife, a peripheral, silently reclusive figure, dies giving birth to Towle's still-born child. The protagonist's mother similarly retreats from view upon learning of the bobby-soxer's death. Like Bunty's mother in *Eagle Eye,* she becomes a latter-day Lady of Shallot: "'I can see it all from my [bedroom] window. It's just that I cannot always wake'" (*B-S,* 199).

The protagonist takes to the heights for a very different reason. Like Bunty Bronstein's, hers is a temporary retreat so as to gain a sharper perspective on who she is and wants. When Towle terminates their collaboration, having drafted a version of the play that, in her mind, glosses over Leo's ambiguities, the protagonist frequents the third floor of her grandmother's house—once Leo's domain—"strain[ing] toward Leo with whatever empathy [she] had been born with, or learned" (*B-S,* 217). Once she had shrunk from the furthest reaches of the house, the Captain's walk, "that enclosure, reached by a last twist of steps from the third floor. . . . where your steps could only circle and never stretch" (*B-S,* 80). But this had been Leo's chosen vantage point on the town, the world she never left. Wearing a pair of Leo's shoes and gazing at the town through the dead woman's opera glasses, the protagonist "watch[es] this theater of the ordinary with the eye of one who had never traveled" (*B-S,* 236). No blinding revelations about Leo result: "Leo remains—Leo" (*B-S,* 280). In medical terms she may be termed a freak, a monster,—not, however, "'With a capital M'"; she is "'Only the ordinary monster we all are'" (*B-S,* 251).

At the novel's end the adult narrator again gazes down on the town, this time from the cemetery hill. In the intervening years she has traveled extensively as an actress; still, the "theater of the ordinary" remains the most engrossing: "I'm only a geisha of words, speaking to please, and by rote. But the real gangplank, the riskiest—isn't that one's life?" (*B-S,* 276). Years earlier Towle called her "'a beginning animal'" (*B-S,* 158); she is no less of one now, still listening to that inner imperative to "Externalize" (*B-S,* 93) the self and the world.

The novel ends on a characteristically nonconclusive note. If there is a constant in the protagonist's life it is, paradoxically, to go on waiting and observing, in the realization that "All lives are legendary. I haven't yet gathered in all the threads of my own, nor will I ever" (*B-S,* 281). The novel is full of ungathered threads, of lives that remain almost as elusive as Leo's. *The Bobby-Soxer* celebrates its protagonist's avidity to read the "language of appearance" (*B-S,* 45) despite—or, perhaps, because of—the opacity and the fluidity of character. In this novel, as in *Textures of Life, Queenie* and *Eagle Eye,* coming-of-age necessarily means coming to see more clearly both the potential range and the real limitations of one's perceptions.

3

False Entries

Calisher describes *False Entry* (1961), her first novel, and *The New Yorkers* (1969), her fourth, as "one chronicle, approachable from either end, fitting together like the halves of an almond and publishable as *A Single Story*" (*H*, 65). At the heart of both novels is an upper-middle-class Jewish family: in *False Entry*, the English Goodmans; in *The New Yorkers*, the American Mannixes, who play, in terms of plot, a significant off-stage role in the earlier novel. The novels also pair off formally and thematically: both are expansive narratives, spanning several decades. Their adult protagonists undergo similarly difficult and protracted transitions from stasis to foreward movement only after confronting painful memories.

The past all but obliterates the fictional present in *False Entry*, cast, for the most part, in the form of its protagonist's memoir. Pierre Goodman, a man in his early forties, has steered clear of real intimacy. He prefers to make "false entry" into other people's lives under false pretenses or assuming identities not his own—not for any malicious purpose, but (he tells himself) as an exercise in alternatives:

> In each little world I remained for a time, trailing my mists but warmed, always in the end moving on. There were times when I merely "visited" as it were, for an evening. . . . For more complicated excursions . . . I rehearsed my disguises more thoroughly, sinking myself well in the role beforehand, like an actor with a two-hour makeup to apply. . . . These were to be my tricks of leisure, my avocation. . . . (*FE*, 395–96)

Beyond Pierre's intellectual savoring of "the protean gap between what is and what might be" (*FE*, 49) lies a motivating fear of self-disclosure, for "beneath it all, the self, that naked contemplative, [lies] safe in his grove" (*FE*, 396).

Until his latest false entry into the household of Judge Mannix and his daughter Ruth, Pierre—like Bunty in *Eagle Eye*— maintained "the free falcon stare of the outsider" (*FE*, 63). Now, having fallen in love with Ruth, Pierre must decide whether to remain "a vicarious man"

(*FE*, 398) or to commit himself to her without subterfuge. Gifted—or cursed—with a photographic memory, he makes that his "harnessed 'familiar'" (*FE*, 57) and begins writing his memoir, hoping "that my hand, trailing in the stream of myself, will produce me" (*FE*, 39). Divided into four sections—"Innocence," "Compromise," "False Entry," and "Entry"—the novel charts the significant episodes in his journey from solitary detachment to an involved life.

"Innocence" begins with Pierre's earliest memories of a happy childhood in England and ends, in a small American Southern town. The section's extremes of place and tone create a fairy tale–like atmosphere. For the first ten years of his life, Pierre's is a seamlessly happy existence: his Edenic world is an upper-middle-class English family in, appropriately enough, Golders Green, London. There, the son of the Goodmans' widowed dressmaker, Pierre soaks up the "generalized kindness" they bestow on "accessory benevolences" (*FE*, 11) such as himself. He especially values his role as silent confidant to the family's aged matriarch, Frau Goodman.

At age ten, however, he and his mother emigrate to Tuscana, a dreary small town in Alabama. There, in the bleak household of his ailing aunt and her taciturn husband, Pierre silently grieves for his lost paradise. The trauma of separation from all that he loves will have long-lasting reverberations. Helpless to return to his spiritual home, he salvages his role as Frau Goodman's "listener *manqué*" (*FE*, 12); for thirty years Pierre draws emotional sustenance from being the unconfiding confidant to others' cherished memories.

Two distinct yet parallel experiences—in one, Pierre is the confidant; in the other, the confider—harden the adolescent's conviction that "the only safe confidant was myself" (*FE*, 123). His only friend in Tuscana is a fellow innocent: Johnny Fontana, from the wrong side of the tracks, who idealizes the respectable middle-class families of the town just as Pierre does the Goodmans. But the longer Pierre listens to Johnny's paean to a Tuscana "golden as a Breugel" (*FE*, 22), the more uneasy he becomes. His own golden vision may be as transparently false, especially if he should articulate it.

The loss of both visions marks for Pierre the end of childhood. Johnny's mythical Tuscana vanishes the night he and Pierre stumble onto a Klan meeting. The Southern-born Johnny is horrified not by the fact that his heroes are Klansmen but by the discovery that their leader is Semple, whom he sees as evil incarnate. Even so, Johnny's hunger for the ideal is undiminished:

In essence what he said was that Tuscana was not like other places; it was a town gone wrong. . . . And Semple was all its evil. . . . Elsewhere there were towns . . . strong as cathedrals, resting on the holy framework he gave them. (*FE*, 65)

On the surface, Pierre's disillusionment is far less dramatic. When his mother announces that she is to marry her sister's widower, George Higby, Pierre despairs of ever returning to "the place that [he] had chosen as the receptacle of [his] innocence" (*FE*, 459), the Goodman household. For a few moments, however, aided by his photographic memory, he effects an imaginative return: "I talked on, remembering, my tongue never fast enough for what I saw" (*FE*, 26). His memory is so inclusive and his yearning so intense that he does manage to obliterate the present—until, that is, his mother's voice breaks in:

> at the wee end of the telescope, my mother cried out, and came forward. She cannot reach me, I thought, for now I am with them. . . . but the long arm grew and reached me, shaking, shaking . . . and all was smashed. (*FE*, 27)

His private world made public, Pierre believes it is lost forever: "It was because someone else knew now. . . . Someone else had a paring of me" (*FE*, 27). He resolves never again to speak his inmost thoughts to another; only the listener is safe.

The teenage Pierre of the novel's second section, "Compromise"—intellectually gifted and scornfully aloof from the drab mediocrity of Tuscana—distances himself from his parents' drably correct lives: "I saw how life was blunting both [their] inner and outer edges . . . and despised them for allowing it" (*FE*, 73). When his mother asks that Pierre legally change his name to his uncle's, George Higby, Pierre rebels against what he sees as an untenable compromise with mediocrity. He substitutes "Pierre Goodman," on the legal petition, believing that by the time the change is legalized he will have left for a northern college. Instead, he is in the courtroom with his mother, who suffers a stroke, apparently as a result of the shock, and Pierre leaves Tuscana— at her request.

Choosing "Pierre Goodman" over "George Higby," Pierre repudiates his mother, "the natural, the female guardian of the philistine" (*FE*, 144), and his uncle's seemingly colorless personality. He also— in this, his first conscious false entry—takes on (albeit, unconsciously) a new, composite identity. Pierre never knew his own purportedly charming but dissolute father. As a child, he was enthralled by Frau Goodman's charismatic brother, Pierre, "a Merlin of talents" (*FE*, 129): the only person, clearly, who could measure up to the boy's unarticulated dream of a father. The elder Pierre's freedom from binding relationships especially intrigues the boy: "how canny a dilettante one had to be if one could not trust oneself to be loved or saw its limits too clearly—how careful, just in time, to move on" (*FE*, 136).

The young Pierre never learns his idol's patronymic. His choice of "Goodman" underscores conflicting loyalties: the "Pierre" in him yearns for the romantic, the protean; the "Goodman," for enveloping domesticity. This dual attraction continues into adulthood when Pierre insinuates himself into other people's lives, careful, however, to keep the exit well in sight.

At the conclusion of Part II, Pierre has successfully freed himself from familial ties: "now [he] was left to find out what that freedom was" (*FE*, 202). Before leaving Tuscana, however, he realizes what kind of a father he could have had in George Higby: "a man I could have asked, whom I could have trusted never to ask—the confidant I could have had" (*FE*, 206). All these years, Pierre had taken his uncle's laconism as a sign of "inner aridity" (*FE*, 201); now he comprehends

> why he moved so carefully, spoke so seldom. He was a man so undeceived about others that he could say little that would not hurt or repel them, who ... dared move only from modulation to modulation because he had so little self-deception on which to depend. (*FE*, 199)

Before confronting even more painful memories in the third section, "False Entry," Pierre takes "Time up for air," returning to the present, which he now sees in another light:

> Memory, though still the powerful vehicle I could not desert, was not safety, and had never been. The present, stealing along my veins even now like some analgesic midnight sun, was the reverse of the medal. (*FE*, 244)

Before returning to his narrative, Pierre writes to Ruth—"*I may have something to show you*" (*FE*, 246)—thus opening the door a crack to the present and beyond. Still, he is ambivalent: "She is the present ... and I am afraid of them both" (*FE*, 246).

When Pierre resumes the memoir, at the beginning of the third section, it becomes clear why he needed a breather: he is about to recount his most dramatic false entry, one that had tragic consequences. When a college junior, Pierre returned to Tuscana to visit his dying mother. His visit corresponds with a Grand Jury investigation into the disappearances of two black boys seven years earlier, the night Pierre and Johnny watched Tuscana's Klansmen gather outside town.

Thanks to his total recall, Pierre becomes the state's star witness. Assuming Johnny's persona, Pierre gives false, yet true, testimony: "I speak as Johnny would, using what he did, what he knew" (*FE*, 325). He does so for justice's sake—in essence, a private justice: Pierre is most intent on avenging Johnny's—and, by extension, his own—loss of innocence. The Klan has its revenge, however: a bullet intended for Pierre kills his uncle, thus hastening his mother's death.

For the next twenty years, Pierre finds a refuge from "the real multiplicity of the world outside" (*FE*, 377) as a resident staff worker for an encyclopedia, where the only entries are impersonal and factual. In his spare time, he physically visits the lives of strangers, having first researched each as assiduously as he does his encyclopedia entries:

> What I came for was . . . the same inexplicable sensation. The control that comes from foreknowledge. . . . Detachment—I take my place, specious as it is, in their midst. . . .
> But above all, a sense of the utter secrecy of myself. For when one is among people on false terms, then no matter what emotion one gives them, one really gives nothing away. (*FE*, 119–20).

In time, however, "the warmth once so admired from the window frame . . . no longer satisfied" (*FE*, 405). Posing as a friend of Judge Mannix's deceased son, Pierre finds in that household the intellectual and emotional "complication" (*FE*, 405) he relishes. His intimate knowledge of the family comes from the deathbed reminiscences of Walter Stern: another lonely, fatherless boy, who idolized the Mannixes as Pierre did the Goodmans. Pierre's initial impressions solidify the Goodman-Mannix connection:

> I no longer hear what they have said or what they have not said, all drowned in what I have come for. Behind me it sounds in all its solid C major, the haven note of the household that was never anywhere else, that was never anywhere (*FE*, 417).

But six months after his first visit, he realizes that unless he leaves he will soon hear the house "in all its restless undertones beneath the public one" (*FE*, 424). In spite of his determination to remain the disinterested observer, he is falling in love with the Judge's thirty-one-year-old daughter, Ruth. When they finally make love, Pierre experiences a momentary sense of innocence and paradise regained: of complete and unself-conscious union—true entry—with another.

But as soon as they physically separate Pierre thinks: *"I could love her, if it were not for myself"* (*FE*, 437), the self that has dreaded real intimacy. That fear only intensifies when Pierre learns that even though Ruth knows him to be an imposter—any friend of her brother would have known of his deafness—she nevertheless loves and trusts him. As in the Biblical story of Adam and Eve, Pierre is suddenly ashamed of his nakedness, literal and emotional, and, in fleeing Ruth, banishes himself from that second lost paradise. That very night he begins his memoir: the "long skin-dive into the nether regions of myself, learning to move about in the intense, direct element of motive, which underlies the upper atmosphere of acts" (*FE*, 214).

Three months later, the memoir completed, Pierre returns to that upper region. When Ruth sends a telegram in her stead—*"Sorry, guess I'm funking it. Better off on your own. Both of us"*—Pierre flies to the Goodmans' London home: "A man who has no person, hunts a place" (*FE*, 447). Revisiting this place is a necessary exorcism. For a few moments in that much-changed household, Pierre becomes a child again, reenacting a familiar ritual with the now ancient Frau Goodman: "It was my last impersonation, as it had been my first, but I could not know this; we do not lightly assist at the death of the child we were" (*FE*, 472). Pierre's return permits him finally to reconcile fragmented selves: the child in him, convinced that love is a place, with the man, reaching out to a person; the confidant, allowing himself only false entries into other lives, with the confider, eager to hand Ruth a "paring" of himself—the memoir.

There is, in fact, a moment of synchonization when child and man, false and true entries merge. When asked his name—the Goodmans remember him only as "Dora's boy" (*FE*, 477)—Pierre replies: "'I was named for my father. My name is George.' I said in requiem, '"George Higby"'" (*FE*, 478). Pierre's true entry—the turning point when listener becomes speaker—has begun with a lie that is fundamentally the truth. Over twenty years have passed since Pierre stood silently in Tuscana's courtroom and heard his new name made public; now, however, he publicly lays claim to a real, not a fantasy, father figure.

For almost thirty years an essential part of Pierre was like a fairy tale character in a deep sleep. Now, upon his return to a real rather than idealized family—having "seen what happens to a live house" (*FE*, 479)—and, more crucially, having acknowledged his spiritual parentage, Pierre has broken the spell. Upon his return to New York, he reaches out toward his present, toward Ruth, with a telegram: "No, not better off on our own" (*FE*, 479). She, too, has painful disclosures (not revealed until *The New Yorkers*) which, encouraged by Pierre, she recounts over the phone. Pierre is the confidant, but not as before: "I listened—and I was the friend" (*FE*, 483).

The catalyst for Pierre's memoir was the realization that he could love Ruth if he were other than an interested, but fundamentally detached, observer. His imaginative and literal returns to the past have effected a radical reevaluation of himself:

> [A]ll my life I had despised my own consciousness, taking the gradual thickening of its complexities always for dishonor. . . . Now came to me, in a slackening so great it must be happiness, that the heart doomed to watch itself feel is not less worthy. (*FE*, 445)

Even though it has destroyed "those green places where we can no longer lay ourselves down," that consciousness is the "substitute glory" (*FE*, 484). If it were not for that ability to stand outside himself and critically, objectively, record and analyze his motives and actions, Pierre would be helpless to break the pattern of vicarious living in which he had become trapped. Three of the novel's four major sections conclude with Pierre's walking away from, rather than toward: at the end of "Innocence," Pierre, at Johnny's command, leaves the older boy alone to grieve for his lost paradise; at the end of "Compromise," he is leaving Tuscana, at his mother's command; at the end of "False Entry," his uncle dead, his mother soon to die, he is about to leave Tuscana, never to return.

Within that general pattern of flight, there is, however, another, opposing pattern of entries that culminates in a movement at once literal and symbolic, when Pierre walks to the door to welcome Ruth's—and his own—"formal entry into the enclosure" (*FE*, 484).

Throughout the novel, doors function as a controlling metaphor. They have had a special significance for the younger Pierre: privileged access to some private world. It hardly seems coincidental—though perhaps not conscious on Calisher's part—that his mother's name, Dora Cross, suggests a pun: door across. It is, after all, she who provides Pierre access to the Goodmans. Once established as an appendage in the household, a literal door—that leading into Frau Goodman's suite—looms large in his imagination. It is on that threshold that the young boy stands, balancing a tray with wine and glass, anticipating the ritualistic exchange and the old woman's reminiscences. It is just outside that door that Pierre, on the day he learns he is to leave the Goodmans, hurls himself and the tray down a flight of stairs: an enraged response to—and physical representation of—his sense of banishment.

As an adolescent in Tuscana, Pierre finds a pale substitute for that lost world in the town's library, whose spinster librarian permits him private entrance:

> a narrow, wisteria-hidden jalousie. . . . As I . . . entered, I stood still for a minute, flooded with a sudden peculiar comfort. For a moment, standing there in the flattery of secret privilege, I was washed inward, past some gate, inside. (*FE, 30*)

Pierre now understands that such moments of comfort "were always to be connected with secrecy, with some hermetic privilege that was mine alone" (*FE, 30*).

Doors have yet another significance for Pierre, one connected not with his yearning for privileged access or secret enclosure but with his "appetite for alternatives" (*FE, 177*), for those moments when dualities seem to exist in a harmonious equilibrium: "that outdoors-indoors blend which always excited him followed him in like the heady admixture of life itself, and held him poised" (261). At the novel's end, Pierre once again stands poised before a door; this time, however, anticipating true entry, with Ruth, into "the great enclosure of the norm" (*FE, 165*):

> Like a host of Atlases we hold each other up, who cannot hold. The sin is not to try; the illusion—to exalt what we can do. Deliver us to one another—to ourselves.
> The bell rings. It is she. I walk toward her, bringing her my paring. This is the entry. Nothing concludes but the power to go on. We walk toward. The ordinary, advancing like lichen, covers us all. (*FE, 484*)

Like the great majority of Calisher's protagonists, Pierre wholeheartedly embraces what he once feared: a life buffeted by chance and change.

That same movement from statis to mobility shapes *The New Yorkers*. Here, however, it is a family—or, more accurately, its survivors, father and daughter—undergoing the transition from false to true entry. The novel spans a twelve-year period in the Mannix household, from a death, in 1943, to a marriage, in 1955: from the near demise of a family, through a period of withdrawal and, in a sense, false entries, to true entry "in full view of the city" (*NY, 3*).[1]

The novel opens with a lyrical, sepia-toned description of the Mannix house as seen by passersby:

> rich and poor, alike on the way to their hives, walked slower at the sight of the Mannix house, four stories above the stoop, all softly Florentined

> from within by light which seemed to come from another clime. . . . The house was one they had once owned or visited, or dreamed. And afterwards, they thought they remembered it. (*NY*, 3)

Throughout the novel, the house will work its magic on various characters who have in common only their gravitation to the house and its inhabitants. It is for visitors what the Goodman family was for Pierre in *False Entry*: an "ever acquisitively generous" (*NY*, 70) household in which intellect, wit, and a comfortable elegance reign. For Judge Simon Mannix, that house is much more: "'A moral entity. . . . In a howling world'" (*NY*, 7). When, at the narrative's outset, that "howling world" theatens to engulf his household, the Judge determines to make it a fortress impenetrable to attack. All the while, the house's public identity remains unperturbed. This duality—public versus private life—is the first of a series: language versus act, past versus present, combatant versus noncombatant.

Part I, "The Crime Circle," spans an eight-year-period (1943–1951). Following the initial act of violence that sets the plot in motion, the drama turns inward, focusing primarily on the Judge's private grappling with pain and with his decision to bury the truth. At the peak of his career, the fifty-two-year-old Judge has returned home from a testimonial dinner in his honor to find his wife Mirriam, cradled in her lover's arms, shot dead by their daughter. It was, in essence if not in fact, a suicide, but the Judge can only intuit that, having resolved never to question Ruth—or to allow her to speak—about that night.

Only in the novel's penultimate chapter, when Ruth finally speaks, do we learn the details of that night. The twelve-year-old Ruth, awakened in the middle of the night by her first menses, had witnessed a struggle between Mirriam and her lover:

> She was trying to get him to murder her. But he wouldn't. . . "Get the gun!" She said that to *him*. . . . "Help me!" she said—"*escape*." . . . In monstrous love and tenderness, I gave her the hate she could get from no one else. (*NY*, 503)

Ruth acted as her suicidal mother's instrument, so now the Judge makes himself Ruth's—"He had a babe, a jewel he must keep hidden" (*NY*, 61). And when Mirriam's lover ensures that the death appear to be a suicide, both father and daughter are safe from public—though not private—judgment.

Immediately following Mirriam's death, the Judge retires from office and turns all his adjudicating impulses inward, substituting thought and language for action. The repeated act of lying about

Mirriam's death takes its toll: the Judge experiences a physical oppression—a sensation of never being naked—that he finally dispels by a kind of magical formulation or distillation of the truth:

Lying on his bed, he had spent hours or seconds of non-time fussing lucidly over it, finding that although at first he had formulated the names as they appeared in the death notice: *Mirriam Sheba Mendes, mother of Ruth Zipporah and David Daniel Mannix*—he was not required to do this, but could say simply: Mirriam, Ruth; my daughter, my wife. And he wasn't required to say *kill*, for that implied intent of which he was ignorant. When he comprehended that he was to say only what he himself knew for sure, then the words were given him, as in the Bible. *My daughter Ruth has shot my wife, her mother Mirriam.* Next he was given to understand that he might drop the "has"—for time passes, and the "wife and mother" also—for the dead must rest. "Daughter" he must keep, as he would keep her. (*NY,* 116)

For a time, the Judge associates the substitution of language for action with a premature old age: "instead of living life, he was living an idea of life" (*NY,* 146). When, however, he involves himself in rescuing refugees from war-torn Europe, he is rejuvenated not merely by the work itself, but by the realization that "'Talk *is* action'":

For where his own father would have gone into "rescue work" as what one did naturally for history and posterity, he himself had done so . . . as his only chance, crannied between wars to share right *in* action. Only to find that the old-fashioned blood-and-thunder vision of action as supreme over thought . . . had changed for him and others. (*NY,*146)

In the climactic chapter of Part I, the Judge once again considers life in the public arena, but like Pierre Goodman he is determined to keep "the self, that naked contemplative, safe in his grove" (*FE,* 396). His liaison to the world—indeed, his designated proxy—is Edwin Halecsy. Strongly reminiscent of Pierre Goodman—poor and fatherless, possessed of a keen intelligence and a determination to rise above his meager beginnings—Halecsy quickly becomes an appendage to the Mannix household and, to some extent, a surrogate son. When he first appears in the novel, he has been the Judge's eager apprentice for seven years and has just completed his first year in law school. The Judge proposes a new relationship: Halecsy is to be his "'confidential secretary'" (*NY,* 190)—"'When I talk to myself, you will hear'" (*NY,* 192)—and his proxy, publishing under his own name the Judge's law articles.

The notion of proxies is important in the novel, corresponding roughly to impersonations in *False Entry*. It occurs early on, in a conversation between the Judge and Oldney, an elderly mentor, about the Civil War practice of hiring substitutes. The distinction between combatant and noncombatant is a painfully personal one for the Judge: like Olney, he has never seen battle. Unlike Olney, he has never come to terms with his exemption from the front line, with the knowledge that, first as a son, now as a father, he belongs to, in Olney's words,

> "Families that go on breeding behind the lines, or in the intervals. Or have men that for some reason or other get saved out. . . . Parlor breeds . . . but there's no shame to it, when it's accident. Somebody has to sit and talk. And breed." (*NY,* 17)

However ambivalent the Judge may feel about his own status as noncombatant, he is nonetheless determined that his family remain "behind the lines," and, to that end, is willing to allow others to fight his battles. The Judge's first and most dramatic proxy is Mirriam's lover, who tampers with the crime scene, making the death seem a suicide. Halecsy also functions as the Judge's substitute. Even eight years after Mirriam's death, the Judge feels the need to keep a low profile: through Halecsy, he has the satisfaction of seeing his work—though not his name—made public. Halecsy is also a more personal kind of buffer: the confidential secretary who, in the Judge's words, "'would see to it that I don't confide'" (*NY,* 190)—even, or most especially, to himself.

On one level, Part II, "Families Behind the Lines," mirrors Part I: a party followed by a late-night scene of violence in the house. The Judge's dinner party is a kind of coming-out party, a private celebration of his recent decision to leave, if only emotionally and symbolically, the confines of his study. It is also a public celebration: if the Judge's home is his religion, then the dinner party is a holy, though not solemn, rite, confirming the specialness of that household. The guests are a disparate group, united under "clouds of pseudo family feeling" (*NY,* 300).

Later that night, however, the Judge learns, for the second time, how fragile his separate peace is. Ruth and Halecsy are the only ones awake in the sleeping house, just as almost nine years before, her mother and lover were. In an earlier conversation Halecsy had misinterpreted an enigmatic statement of the Judge's which convinces him that the Judge, his hero and moral paradigm, murdered his wife. Halecsy then takes out his sense of betrayal and rage against his mentor on Ruth. He rapes—Ruth offers no resistance—and brutally beats her. Halecsy believes he is striking out at the real murderer through a proxy, the person the Judge most cherishes; Ruth—now, as then, in her menses—accepts physical punishment for that nine-year-old act. Once again, the Judge comes to his daughter's aid.

The past has—and has not—repeated itself. Ruth has, in some sense, replayed that scene in which her mother was the willing victim; the judge has reenacted his role as protector. The repetition, with significant variations, is a necessary one. The violence has been cathartic for them both: Ruth finally breaks the charged, guilt-ridden silence between them:

> "I am the missing person. I can't pretend anymore." . . . Now that she'd told him what he wanted to know—that she knew what she was—she was old enough to watch a man cry. (*NY*, 391)

Throughout the novel, Ruth has been at the center of the drama, but so securely encased in a self-protective shell that she seems, indeed, "'the missing person." Following her mother's death, Ruth made ballet her refuge; its rigidly circumscribed steps are her defense against chaos, physical and emotional. Ballet is also an escape from language, from speaking the truth; there is safety and control only "in the dry marionette words of the ballet, those light, eighteenth century improvisations for the clockwork of the limbs" (*NY*, 506). Not until the closing pages of the novel does Ruth find her own voice; in so doing, she releases both herself and her father from their constricted lives.

The novel's concluding section, Part III, which takes place three years after the Judge's dinner party, is ironically entitled "Beautiful Visits"—ironic in light of its series of wrenching, but necessary, revelations. The climactic encounter is between the Judge and Ruth. Having regained her voice, Ruth becomes her father's judge when she learns that once again her father tried to ward off painful realities—again, by means of a proxy. Ruth's friend since childhood, Walter Stern (the man whose reminiscences Pierre Goodman drew on in *False Entry*), has just died; before his death he destroyed a letter Mirriam Mannix entrusted to him. The letter would settle any doubts the Judge has had as to whether or not David was truly his son, but he asks Walter to destroy it: "'There *are* some things I'd rather not know'" (*NY*, 438).

When Ruth learns, too late, of Walter's fatal operation and of the letter's destruction, she becomes the accuser: "'You used him. As a . . . as a—' again she tried. 'Mercenary. To do your own job'" (*NY*, 448). Ruth feels doubly bereft—of both Walter and, via the letter, of her mother: "'I thought—she might tell me once again, from her own mouth. That I—would do her no injury. Did her—none'" (*NY*, 449).

In the wake of Ruth's angry leavetaking, the Judge hears her unspoken accusation—that he has used her all these years as a buffer between himself and Mirriam:

> It was like coming out of madness—of murder, or a bed—of love, to realize the other person. Who had now made him drop every item of the silent entente which the two of them had lived.
> *Don't you know yet, Father? How you used me?* (*NY*, 449)

He then addresses his dead wife:

> Mirriam! . . . There was no time to mourn you, until now. I had to mourn her. That's how I used her, surely? She herself said. Or didn't say. Now she's gone . . . I can mourn you. (*NY*, 455)

In much the same way that Pierre spoke the name "George Higby" in requiem for the flesh-and-blood father he could have had, so the Judge speaks his wife's name, able at last to admit the extent of his loss. For him, as or Pierre, it is a moment of reconciliation with the past.

In the novel's penultimate chapter, both father and daughter "walk toward" (*NY*, 516) others: Ruth, to the friend since childhood whom she will soon marry; the Judge, to his lover, formerly Ruth's dance mistress. But even as they parallel they dramatically contrast with each other: Ruth, who had formerly sought refuge from speech in movement, finds her release in language; the Judge, for whom speech has long been a form of action, finds his in physical movement.

Just as, in the conclusion of *False Entry*, Pierre brings the memoir, his "paring," to Ruth, so now Ruth makes her true entry by becoming the confider: "'I'm beginning to speak. I won't be the mystery any more'" (*NY*, 517). The peripheral figure, no longer a "watcher from the wings" (515), finally comes center stage, becoming in life what she could never be in ballet: "The Assoluta" (*NY*, 466).

The Judge also comes out of hiding. For him, however, the simple, physical movement forward constitutes true entry: "Action is the best rhetoric of all" (*NY*, 459). By now almost totally confined to a wheelchair, he manages, by sheer will power, it seems, to walk alone, unaided: "'Yes—I'm out in public'" (*NY*, 465). His dependency on proxies, on buffers, has come to an end.

By the novel's end, the Judge has radically revised his notion of what constitutes public and private life, and, in so doing, has broken free from a self-imposed confinement, at once literal and emotional:

> What was "public" life? The access of each organism into the current, and its submission to it, held all the drama of life. . . . I am wounded, but I live. I am in healing—and shall never get over it. (*NY,* 558–59)

That act of capitulation has overtones of a religious experience, of finding oneself by losing oneself in a greater reality. For Calisher, however, what is most sacred is what is most human: the warp and woof of the textures of life, "[t]he ordinary, advancing like lichen, [that] covers us all" (*FE,* 484), the current of histories, private and communal, "that we were all of us gliding through" (*NY,* 559).

4

Solo Flights

In the works previously examined, Calisher's protagonists enter what they had once feared: "the great enclosure of the norm" (*FE,* 165). There are, however, very different kinds of extraditions and initiations in some of Calisher's fictions. In the novellas *The Railway Police* (1966), *Survival Techniques* (1985), and the novel, *On Keeping Women* (1977), the protagonists cut themselves loose from the ties that once bound them to the textures of everyday life, shedding their conventional lives like dead skins. The unnamed protagonists of the novellas speak out through their actions, sloughing off possessions and identities to become literal vagrants, while the aptly named Lexie in *On Keeping Women* finds her liberation in language.

The heroine of *The Railway Police*—an attractive, financially independent social work supervisor—has, in her own mind, lived a life of pretense: since adolescence she has literally concealed "the felony of [her] private difference"—congenital baldness. The novella opens on her spur-of-the-moment decision not only to divest herself of wigs but also to "be out of the organized world" (*RP,* 15)—to become a street person.[1] The train has just pulled into, appropriately enough, Providence, when the railway police apprehend a ticketless passenger, a young vagrant, "just a hairsbreadth too unshaven" (*RP,* 9). The protagonist, impeccably groomed and polished, from her hat and coiffed wig to her gloves, pinpoints and embraces what sets him apart:

> It takes keeping up, any posture of what you are not, takes a sense of fitness to the point of fashion, and the vagrant won't bother with that sort of thing, not for that purpose, he's too honest for it, or else he wants to be spotted; maybe it's his very function in life to wander about thus exposed so that others may find their signals in him. (*RP,* 9)

With "a kind of suffragette swelling, part yearning and part vengeful" (*RP,* 15), she rejects "orthodox womanhood" (*RP,* 4) and sets out to become not only a vagrant but also, and more significantly, just such a signal to others.

68

Even as she takes immediate, practical steps to divest herself of possessions and identity—her first decisive move is to discard her wig box—she, like so many of Calisher's characters, breaks free of the past only after immersing herself in it. Through memory, she charts the hitherto submerged current that has led to this decision. Not surprisingly, the matter of her baldness dominates three particular episodes from the past.

In her youth, she broke off an engagement with a man for whom her baldness—and possibly that of the child she was carrying—posed no problem: it was a simple physical fact. Upon his refusal to marry her if she aborted their child—"'Children can learn to be bald'" (*RP,* 22)—she rejects both his condition of marriage and its accompanying assertion. To her mind, "To be acceptable, such decisions must come to the bald—from the bald" (*RP,* 23). In the years that follow, she, like Pierre Goodman in *False Entry,* remains solitary. Feeling herself to be a private outcast, she dedicates herself to society's outcasts.

In the second decisive encounter, the protagonist is, for a brief time, exhilarated by the possibility of real intimacy. She falls in love not at first sight but at first hearing a man in an art gallery, anxious to purchase a Picasso, rhapsodize about baldness:

> "Kept thinking of it all the time I was away. Most of all in Bangkok. Monks with shaved heads, widows too. . . . Modern Giacometti, sculpture without curls. . . . [Y]ou've never seen the glory of the unadorned human head before." (*RP,* 25)

Here, at last, is a man who might treasure what the protagonist has—or, more accurately, lacks. Still, she keeps her baldness a secret until, one night in bed, she joins him completely naked from head to toe. Believing she has shaved her head for him, he proceeds, though clearly appalled, with love making—until, that is, she nuzzles her head against his lips, literally rubbing his face in the bare facts.

The protagonist then makes a quasi-religious pilgrimage to Bangkok, to those shaved-headed monks and widows. However, she quickly rejects "group solutions to both philosophical problems and practical ones" (*RP,* 38–39). It is only when she is no longer consciously searching for signs that she finds one in a pariah dog that, she remembers, "rolled his eyes up at me, unmistakably me, and slowly thumped his tail. . . . He lifted his coattails to me . . . in signal" (*RP,* 41). She returns to New York, to her old routines, forgetting the moment until, that day on the train, "One of [the vagrant's] coattails flipped up" (*RP,* 8) in a signal she now understands.

When she makes her debut as a vagrant, she does so on her own, idiosyncratic terms. Neither an unimaginative pragmatist, like her first lover, nor too much the aesthete, like her second, she is, rather, a pragmatic aesthete:

> I took a plaid car-blanket of consoling warmth and color, and a change of inner and outer clothing. . . . At the last moment I add a short veil of gauze.
> The veil was connected with a slight ambition of mine . . . For it's entirely possible to be both honest and frivolous. . . . So, for Paris in the spring, I carried gauze. (*RP*, 56–57)

And in her Abercrombie shoulder bag, the Picasso painting of two bald-headed lovers, a farewell gift from her former lover.

She chooses the setting for her debut—the neighborhood she knew as a social worker—as carefully as she did her apparel:

> The viaduct is a particularly coveted one, having at its opposite arch a public convenience, far enough away so that there is no smell. . . . Fires are not allowed by the city, of course, nor sleeping, but several niches . . . are excellent for either. The neighborhood, too, still a family one though on the fringe . . . attracts a remarkably high class of loiterer. . . . (*RP*, 65)

Until now, she has carefully stage-managed the particulars of her radical transition. But in flight from a policeman determined to help her, she suddenly loses all self-confidence: "it was a long way between signals. . . . I needed to be told that taking something off could be as positive and worthy as putting something on" (*RP*, 70–71). In a Chinese restaurant where she has taken refuge, she finds the reassuring sign when the waiters return her payment for tea in a salad bowl—symbolically now a begging bowl—and bow her out into the street. Returning their bow, she feels herself to be a secular monk: just as others have been her signals, so now she becomes one herself—if only, as yet, to those sympathetic waiters. In the novella's Whitmanesque conclusion she celebrates a universal reciprocity:

> In the inexhaustible doubleness of the world, are there signals everywhere, wild as grass, that unite us? Or must we unite them?
>
>   *   *   *
>
> Come, you narks, cops, feds, dicks, railway police, members of the force everywhere! Run with us! If the world is round, who's running after who? (*RP*, 74)

On this, the symbolically fitting dawn of the first day of spring, she curls up to sleep, back-to-back with a fellow vagrant: "And so—I was born" (*RP*, 74)—not only as a street person, however. In shedding wigs, in giving up the "struggle against the facts like a fly trying to get out of the cosmos" (*RP*, 74), she finally has made peace with her own difference. Now she can assert what once she rejected: "Children can learn to be bald" (*RP*, 74); they (including she) can learn not to disguise difference but to proclaim it, literally out-of-doors.

Almost twenty years after writing *The Railway Police*, Calisher would again explore a solid middle-class citizen's rebirth as a street person in *Survival Techniques*, one of the "little novels" collected in *Saratoga, Hot* (1985). The similarities are striking: both unnamed protagonists find in society's marginal figures the signal they have been waiting for; both view their solo flights not as escapes but as true entries into a more authentic life. The differences are equally striking. The woman in *The Railway Police* has always felt different by reason of her baldness; not so the retired shopkeeper of *Survival Techniques*. He is breaking away not only from a way of life but also from his wife of thirty-five years. His passage, then, from apartment down to street corner is all the more wrenching.

The novella charts his careful transition from one world to another. For most of his adult life, his Vienese burger's wife and his shop-keeper's routine have kept him on the straight and narrowly middle-class path. With retirement, fretting about making ends meet, his perspective on his little world begins to change. He notices first that "There is no other street so brilliantly prime for certain conveniences, for certain people" (*ST*, 173). Four steam heat vents provide warmth in winter; four subway entrances provide toilets and, in inclement weather, shelter "for certain people" (*ST*, 174).

Just as the heroine of *The Railway Police* found her "signal" in a vagrant, so also does the protagonist of *Survival Techniques*. The street's three regulars first attract him by their peculiar dress and demeanor: they do not worry about keeping up appearances or mak-ing ends meet. Even more arresting is their dignity and self-contain-ment: they beg neither for handouts nor for pity.

The protagonist's transition from apartment to street corner is not only gradual; it is also furtive, so as to keep his wife in the dark as long as possible. While she is away working part-time, he spends longer and longer stretches of time on the street, an apprentice watched over by his "three mentors" (*ST*, 186). As his attraction to the street grows, his distaste for apartment life intensifies: "My stay up here was only a hibernation, in which the vision of the street was always with me" (*ST*, 185). That long hibernation ends after a year's deliberation and rehearsal and coincides not, as in *The Railway Police*, with the first day of spring but with the year's first real snowfall: a morning "damp with promise" (188).

While the woman in *The Railway Police* hopes to become a "statement," not a "mystery" (*RP,* 15), the protagonist of *Survival Techniques* aspires to be both: a disquieting and willfully enigmatic presence. He takes refuge, even from his wife, in an impassive silence, refusing either to proclaim or to explain his new vocation. Not surprisingly, the novella concludes not with a celebration of universal kinship but with an admonition from one who is now "outside" (*ST,* 190) to those "who could still pass a body by" (*ST,* 186):

> You yourself were faithful feet. Each day, stopping longer. As if we were the authority to complain to. Dot, dot, your rhythm goes. . . . Dot, dot. And carry your burden on. For we do not beg. If we would beg, you could get past us. I could tell you how.
> The best way is to know nothing about us.
> That is why I keep my eyes lowered. Never look into them. (*ST,* 194)

However enigmatic a figure he is, another of Calisher's protagonists proves to be even more difficult to define. Like the novellas' protagonists, Lexie, the protagonist of Calisher's novel *On Keeping Women,* looks on the life she has led as a hibernation from which she struggles to awake. The novel charts her "voyage into the interior" (*OKW,* 97), a "language-search" (*OKW,* 71) from which Lexie emerges with a newly articulate self bent on travel.

Lexie has parallels both in Calisher's fiction and in her life. Like another Alexandra—the titular Queenie—she was raised to be a "kept woman"—not an old-fashioned courtesan but a suburban wife and mother. Both are native New Yorkers enamored of their city and its promise of boundless possibilities. Both reject ready-made terms of self-definition: female liberation is a goal they both envision achieving individually, not communally. There are, however, significant differences, beginning with the radically different fictional worlds they inhabit. *Queenie*'s is a comic, often surreal universe; that of *On Keeping Women,* a more meditative and densely textured one. Unlike Queenie, a confidant coloratura throughout, Lexie, though her brother sarcastically labels her one (*OKW,* 312), is still in the early, tentative stages of rehearsal.

On Keeping Women addresses the problem of surrendering oneself to the world's vagaries in a more identifiably autobiographical mode. At the outset of her career, Calisher gave fictional shape and autonomy to her childhood and adolescence in the Hester Elkin stories. In *On*

Keeping Women, almost thirty years after the first of the autobiographical stories, she again drew on her own rites of passage.

Lexie is thirty-seven, Calisher's age when, after years of "the house-and-child life—which is a total-flesh-draining, a catatonia of rest for the beaverish brain" (*H,* 29), her first story was published. (The hero of *Survival Techniques* made his debut as a vagrant after thirty-seven years of married life.) Like her fictional counterpart, Calisher wrote poems, never sent out, "in trances of regret for the intellectual life [she] seemed to have lost" (*H,* 29). Lexie, too, is one of two children whose father is a dreamer and whose mother, a pragmatist. In her early twenties, Lexie marries a doctor (Calisher's first husband was an engineer) and she, as did Calisher, sets up housekeeping in a rambling Victorian house on the Hudson, twenty-five miles from the city that nurtured her dreams. Lexie has four children (Calisher, two), one of whom is clearly a fictional counterpart of Calisher's own troubled daughter who committed suicide as a young adult.

Despite these numerous correspondences, the novel is not a fictional autobiography. It is, rather, an extended meditation on the subject of keeping—i.e., organizing, caring for, and keeping down—women. It is, above all else, "One person's manifest—on keeping on" (*OKW,* 313): not merely surviving, but actively nurturing oneself.

The novel's brief introductory section, "On Touching Youth," parallels the conclusion of *The Railway Police* in which its heroine, head bared and exposed to the elements, is poised on the brink of a new life. Lexie lies naked on the riverbank opposite her house in the pre-dawn hours, about to give herself up to the flood of memory so as to answer the question, "Would it get up, this body, toward morning, to creep whitely across the road again; through the door and back into the last eighteen years?" (*OKW,* 3).

Her earliest memories are of fundamentally conflicting messages. On the one hand, both her parents and her brother are determined to "organize" her: to steer her into some safe harbor of conventional life. But she has already absorbed her father's paean to New York: "'With this city—' he'd sigh and never finish. But we knew the end of that sentence: we could do anything, go anywhere" (*OKW,* 6). Although "water was [her] element" (*OKW,* 9), Lexie is soon land-locked. At age twenty she marries Ray, "the most careful of the interns James [her brother] brought home" (*OKW,* 16). They move up the Hudson—"travel parodied" (*OKW,* 306)—to the village of Grand River where, in a Victorian mansion with river rights. Lexie is "organized" only superficially. This first section's conclusion (Lexie's memory of giving birth to her first child, Chessie) foreshadows the novel's conclusion: her sense of giving birth to a new, more acutely self-conscious self:

> At the height, the flames were considerable. . . . "She's one of those who won't scream," I hear the nurse say scornfully. . . . The lower half of my body is almost totally consumed. I am on the point, the absolute point, of learning my lingo. And then I lost it. . . .
> "Scream for *me*, Lexie," [Ray] said.
> So I deliver silently. (*OKW*, 21)

Lexie's silence continues for several years. In the novel's second, and lengthiest, section, "In a Fiery Glade," that takes place some twelve years after the birth of her fourth child, Lexie's life falls into distinct, even predictable stages: first, the total immersion of herself as a mother—"I tremble with selflessness. That candy delight. Stuffed well in, it keeps the language down" (*OKW*, 25). Later, when the children are older, she makes day trips to the city for "Continued Education," both collegiate and extra-marital. Finally, she returns home, burrowing in as preparation for a solo flight.

Laid out this schematically, the novel sounds like another variation on Marilyn French's *The Woman's Room*. Yet neither Calisher nor her protagonist is a "unionist"; in her language search, Lexie goes beyond the jargon, the self-righteous dichotomies of woman as oppressed versus man as oppressor. Given Calisher's highly-valued individuality and her own solitary struggle to find the energy and courage to become a writer, it is not surprising that her fictional counterpart should disdain simplistic formulas and self-pitying credos:

> Awareness—yes, she lives for it. . . . She'd have to define it herself—and not fall in love with it. Only to end up circling that tunnel-of-selflove [sic] which the world called "sensibility," and was particularly happy to attach to the awakenings of her kind. (*OKW*, 313)

She finds the signal she has been waiting for not in any college classroom or in her lovers' beds but, literally, in her own backyard. When a fire next door threatens her own home, "that was the moment. With the house rescued, the children gathered, and the wind blowing away from them. When she knew she would eventually leave" (*OKW*, 68). Seeing that her children could handle the possiblity of one kind of loss, she is assured that they may prove equally adept at handling their mother's departure from the scene.

With the eventuality of leaving now in sight, Lexie becomes more analytically aware of the emotional configurations, private and communal, swirling around her. She sees herself as both an anthropologist and the object of anthropological study: "'I want to voyage into the interior. Mine. . . . And someday . . . maybe I can spell it out'" (*OKW*, 97). In the lengthy concluding episode of "In a Fiery Glade"—a neighbor's party—Lexie arrives at an epiphanic realization; she feels herself both inside and outside the social drama: "'I can watch the double spectacle of myself. . . . And not feel ashamed'" (*OKW*, 153). As with Pierre Goodman of *False Entry*—indeed, as with Calisher herself—"the guilt always attached to the role of observer has finally been annulled . . . by the realization that this is what [she] is here for" (*H*, 76).

On the brink of shedding her old self, she reunites with a former lover, Kevin. After too many hours of steady drinking, Kevin confesses that "'Vital signs [are] not good'" (*OKW*, 171) for an erection. Lexie then initiates oral sex for the first time in her life:

> Now she's face to face with her own willed subdominance .This yearning posture that flows under all household service. . . . As if she's doing a domestic service for him. Relieving him tribally—as nursing mothers gave their extra milk to their men. . . . Blessed to bend the neck, the last vertebral resistance gone crack. I am understanding obedience. Which is the other rhythmic of giving birth. . . .
>
> And at the same time, an ancient childself . . . is suckling. . . . This man-mother—mother him. (*OKW*, 172)

It is a decisive, quintessential act: a final reenactment of her years of "willed subdominace" as a wife and mother before giving birth to a newly articulate self. After Kevin leaves, Lexie's interior journey begins: "she drowns in her own life, upward. Discovers it" (*OKW*, 173).

At this point the novel returns to its opening scene, leaving Lexie motionless on the riverbank. The next two sections, "The Doctor's Prescription" and "Guerilla Games," belong to her husband and children; they, too, are about to leave the family's confine.

Until this point in the narrative, Ray has been a peripheral, silent figure, who has distanced himself emotionally and, for the past four months, physically as well. Laid low by hepatitis while in Spain, he chose to remain on, not only to recuperate but also to gear himself up for what he envisions to be a permanent separation from his family. As Ray's section, "The Doctor's Prescription," opens, he is walking home in the same predawn hour that Lexie lies contemplating her life: "He's thinking of home—a church he no longer believes in—and how to desanctify it" (*OKW*, 185).

Although Ray is this section's center of consciousness, his thoughts are all of Lexie: "His whole life with her had been a conversation. . . .

in which he knew she thought he never said anything" (*OKW*, 208). Even as he empathizes with her compulsion to find her own voice, their great differences exhaust him:

> It hurt him, that she's so aware. It put the burden of being the denser, colder person always on him. . . . Why does he have to get away from it? . . . Because she can always tell him—why. (*OKW*, 207)

On his return to the sleeping house, Ray does, in fact, "desanctify" it, not by words but by a sacriligious act. In the dark hallway outside his and Lexie's bedroom, he embraces and kisses not his wife but his almost grown daughter, Chessie: "On the mouth. but *before* he recognizes her? Or . . . *then?*" (*OKW*, 223). Chessie's knee in his groin sends him running from the house; outside, on the riverbank, the final act of his marriage will take place.

Before that occurs, however, another section, "Guerilla Games," intervenes in which the children take center stage. Three of the four are confident they can weather the family's disintegration: the second oldest, Charles, is college-bound; the middle child, Maureen, is assured of a place in her grandfather's comfortably middle-class house; the youngest, and most disconcertingly precocious, Royal, knows he has a niche in his bachelor uncle's life. Only the eldest child, Chessie, is in real jeopardy.

Chessie is one of Calisher's most complicated and poignant characters: possessed of a piercing intelligence and a sensibility preternaturally attuned to nuance, she is, nonetheless, a painfully vulnerable teenager. If it were not for her, strange to the point of madness, there would be no need for the other three children's guerilla games, ingenious efforts to hide from adults the extent of Chessie's strangeness. In the previous four months—the period of Ray's absence from the family—these games have taken on a new urgency:

> It got to all of them. That Dad, if he was leaving for good, would be taking the house along with him. In similar cases along the road here, the house-as-was had never survived. (*OKW*, 229).

For Chessie, that "house-as-was" is a womb she is loathe to leave: "We're conservationists, [Charles] tells [Maureen and Royal]. . . . And this house is her only preserve" (*OKW*, 228).

Chessie illuminates Lexie's character by both comparison and contrast. For Lexie, as for Ruth in *The New Yorkers*, "language is acts" (*OKW*, 224). Chessie, however, does not have the paradoxically liberating and controlling power of language:

To be all metaphor, inside one's self. . . . [Chessie's] body is all metaphor *physically,* every sensation may be received doubly, triply, or in itself, phantomized. Her own body's the vacuum—full of electronic, electrochemical cries. (*OKW,* 243)

Chessie hears voices but cannot communicate her own; one of her voices, "Lucy," that inner core of lucidity, relays a desperate, terse message: *"Help"* (*OKW,* 242). Otherwise, she expresses herself only in poltergeistlike acts that become more frequent and alarming once she senses her parents' imminent breakup. Her terror and rage manifest themselves in acts symbolic of loss: household items are destroyed, spirited away or deposited in unlikely places; small fires are set, but only when they are sure to be discovered in time.

At the conclusion of "Guerilla Games," it is Chessie who, to her siblings' surprise, takes command. Their own "Lady of Shalott" (*OKW,* 223) leads them down from the house's tower, "down from the alps of childhood, onto the great divide" of adulthood (*OKW,* 256). They, not their parents, are the first to leave—in the family's Volkswagon.

Meanwhile, as the sun rises, Lexie is surfacing from her interior journey. Like the heroine of *The Railway Police* she feels reborn: "You're delivering silently. Women do that. When they've been carrying themselves" (*OKW,* 283). Now, having "recover[ed] from confinement" (*OKW,* 325), she contemplates a new vocation:

But—how to tell the story? Of how people stammer in and out of the dark. In the fiery glades of the families. . . . How to tell the story that's always about to begin? (*OKW,* 325)

Calisher describes a similar scene from her own life in *Herself,* one that adds resonance to Lexie's present and to her open-ended future. Having published her first book and just recently returned from a year in London on a Guggenheim fellowship, she is back home, lying on "the hillside behind the house, head toward the mountain, feet toward the Hudson . . . and all summer reread[ing] books I have never before finished" (*H,* 111). There, Calisher "was growing not a baby, but a book" (*H,* 111).

Although Lexie is all potential at the novel's end, the stage is set for travel and writing. Her nascent self—articulate and solitary—is also, and most important, active rather than passive. She is no longer locked into a rigid, simplistic dichotomy: i.e., the public, powerful, masculine world of acts versus the personal, contemplative feminine world of emotions. At the novel's outset, Lexie is certain that "What she needs most, is to find her own lingo—and have them publish the

Congressional Record in it. At least half the time" (OKW, 19). It is not enough, clearly, to find her own voice; she wants male confirmation:

> Whatever she is has come about because she sees herself as the irrationally mute half of things. As they see her. So that when she does speak, she screams.
>
> And still she waited for [Ray] or one of them or all of them, every cell in her screaming to be found—to be found tragic, equal, necessary. In equal part. (OKW, 314)

Even when envisioning a new, solitary life in the city—"A language thrill went through her—nonsexual" (OKW, 309)—she nevertheless depends on male authority and approbation: "There will they let her be that—objective? Not a gender but a human animal rising?" (OKW, 309).

The crucial turning point occurs when she—like Ruth Mannix in The New Yorkers—comes to believe that language can be action: "If a language is so private it makes people stare—then make it public. Make it a deed" (OKW, 312). In the novel's conclusion, as Lexie rises at last from the riverbank, she no longer thinks in terms of what "they" will or will not let her do; she rises as an exuberantly female "human animal":

> But what has she baubling her ears, hung twinkling in the septum of her nose, indented gemdeep in the forehead—and rubying the warm navel, and sparkling onyx between the legs, in the cleft blur of hair?
>
> It is her body, that sings, an illuminated story—in every pore, hanging in cell-song, that sad jewel, joy. (OKW, 325)

Like the protagonists of the novellas—like Calisher herself—Lexie is "a pilgrim still in progress, shedding fears like skins" (H, 244).

5

Reentries

The protagonists of three other Calisher works—the novellas, *Extreme Magic* (1964) and *Saratoga, Hot* (1984), and the novel, *Standard Dreaming* (1972)—also cast off "fears like skins," but not in preparation for solo flights. After periods of stasis and emotional withdrawal, they reenter that "great enclosure of the norm" from which they had once thought themselves permanently estranged.

In its almost schematic progression, *Extreme Magic*, Calisher's second novella, establishes in a capsulized form the pattern of reentry. For almost ten years Guy Callendar has viewed himself as other people's "extreme," a "triple amputee at the sight of whom even the single-legged may take heart" (*EM,* 184).[1] A house fire killed his wife and children, leaving him survivor and beneficiary. "When the indemnity money came in, thousands upon thousands of it" (*EM,* 179), a mental hospital gently steered him towards its "own necessary fantasy of the goodness and wholeness entirely residual in the world" (*EM,* 183). Now, for seven years, he has known a measure of calm and satisfaction as an antique dealer in upstate New York:

> Sheer luck had . . . nudged him into a modus vivendi whose limits so exactly modulated to his own—one exactly useful to a man able to move on, unable to forgive himself for it. (*EM,* 192–93)

He has also found solace in the "safe visual goodness" (*EM,* 193) of a tree-enclosed space.

In a week's time, the span of the novella, Callendar comes to see himself and the world in very different terms. "Perspective," a key word throughout, first appears when Callendar contemplates his estrangement from ordinary relationships:

> Perspective was what any man carried on his back, not a cross, but an easel to which pictures were supplied slowly, always with an unknown hand. He merely knew better than most what had happened to him. . . . Some men tragedy. . . . pushes altogether out of their sphere. (*EM,* 195)

The first disruption of his well-ordered life occurs when he pays an unexpected visit to an innkeeping couple down the road on their day off. Callendar stumbles into a terrifyingly bizarre scene: Sligo is aiming darts as close as possible to Marion, who stands in front of the bull's-eye. Almost as alarming is Marion's command: "'On't move,'" said the rigid hole of her mouth. . . . He only has two more'" (*EM*, 206). Their Monday ritual ends when, last dart thrown, Sligo slumps into drunken unconsciousness.

Marion is her husband's acquiescent victim—"'We suffer the same'"—who claims she wants to be left alone: "'One gets on better without talking. Pity is fatal'" (*EM*, 210). Even as she asks Callendar not to return because she "'can't afford the perspective,'" she sends out a muted cry for help: "'Is it sick of me? That I stay'" (*EM*, 214). Marion, Callendar's contemporary, reminds him of his earlier self: an extreme case in need not of distant pity but of immediate intervention. He resolves to be there the following Monday.

When he returns to his safe, hemmed-in acreage, Callendar's once fixed perspective is again disturbed, though not unpleasantly, by a sixteen-year-old girl in a bikini. Alden's youth and naïveté are a relief after his nightmarish experience; still, it disconcerts him to learn he has been her "view": "it never struck him that anyone could look in on his solitude" (*EM*, 220). But upon hearing that he has been Alden's "view," he gains a larger, faintly disquieting angle of vision: "He stared . . . at [her] image of this clearing, minuscule in [her] distance, across which [walked] a toy man . . . toy solitary" (*EM*, 222).

When, the next Monday, Callendar and Alden kiss, "He had his perspective. He was the one who was unnatural here" (*EM*, 242)—"here" encompassing the girl and his safe enclosure. Even as they embrace, Callendar has made his choice: "in the silence a quarter-mile from the highway, he could hear within himself the sound of lives, regular as rockets, riding to their Monday smash" (*EM*, 242). What he hears and responds is not only the cruel ritual down the road:

> Around him, real cars whizzed loud as imaginary ones . . . people . . . were on the move. He wanted to . . . call out to them—I'm with you again. I'm part of the violence. (*EM*, 243)

The night before that second Monday, Callendar performs a seemingly mundane domestic chore that both foreshadows and rehearses some great change: "there was really no need for this house-cleaning. But he had an urge to *see* the barn[/house] as empty as it had been when he came" (*EM*, 237). Settling into a sleeping bag on the lawn, Callendar gazes affectionately and nostalgically—his perspective that of an outsider: "The barn was what he loved; he had rescued it" (*EM*, 238)—as it had rescued him.

At the second Monday's "smash" at the inn Callendar finds that Sligo, too, has cleaned house. Standing in the midst of his bar's wreckage, waiting for the sedative Marion has just administered to take effect, Sligo smashes his fist through a glass showcase which holds a purportedly historic but in fact bogus diamond ring. The association between it, himself and his marriage are clear enough: with this final act of destruction, he has passed judgment on three deceptions.

The scene that follows recalls the climactic scenes of *False Entry* and *The New Yorkers:* Pierre and Ruth, finally able to unburden themselves of painful memories, free themselves to move on. To Callendar, her necessary audience, Marion unfolds the twenty-year-old lie that set in motion the "'double dream'" (*EM*, 248). Sligo, a count's Irish groom, passed himself off as his employer to Marion, then a seventeen-year-old student at a posh boarding school. Her guilt stems from having used her background—"'Speech, tastes, needs, a million discriminations people like me . . . didn't even know we were born with'" (*EM*, 253)—as a weapon against Sligo. Callendar responds with a demand he has only recently made of himself: "'Pity *yourself.* . . . So you can leave here. . . . So we can go'" (*EM*, 256).

Waiting for the ambulance that will take Sligo away, the two stand on the riverbank, contemplating a view, literal and symbolic, he had turned his back on:

> they stared into the blind current of the river, and beyond it, into a current wider than it or any harbor, into that vast multiplicity where there might be no sure order of good or evil, but surely a movement. . . . He knew it was there, this force that had flung him out, and drawn or flung him in again, this movement which, like some god of unbelievers . . . both took away, took away—and gave. This was nothing to make either a religion or an unfaith of; it was merely the doctrine . . . which lived somewhere in the tough, central dark of those to whom it happened. For extreme cases there was sometimes—an extreme magic. (*EM*, 258)

If this were a forties' Hollywood movie, violins would swell in the background, rising to a crescendo as the sun sets on the river. Instead, the two turn their backs on the sunset's glow and walk towards the ambulance's "treacherous glare" (*EM*, 259).

At the novella's close Callendar not only fully faces "that vast multiplicity"; he also remembers "How it felt to be only half alone—in all its separate lights and darks"; he is on the verge of reentering, with Marion, "the double dream, [where] one no longer tallied these, or dared" (*EM*, 259).

Callendar's closest fictional counterpart is Pierre Goodman, whose passage from false to true entry repeats itself in so many of Calisher's subsequent works. Both men, in their early forties, survive familial tragedies and shrink from real intimacy. Callendar becomes Marion's confidant much the same way Goodman becomes Ruth's.

Both works end on a note of somber optimism: *False Entry* with Goodman's realization that "Nothing concluded but the power to go on" (*FE*, 484); *Extreme Magic*, with Callendar's remembering "how it felt to be only half-alone" (*EM*, 259).

That same resistence, followed by whole-hearted acquiescence to forward motion, shapes Calisher's brief novel, *Standard Dreaming*, published eight years after *Extreme Magic*. The novel is an extended meditation, its protagonist's "report" (*SD*, 9) to an imagined surgical amphitheater—the novel's internalized "we." The Swiss-born Niels Berners is a middle-aged plastic surgeon living in New York. From his own sense of failure as a father, he has extrapolated a grand construct of the human species *in extremis*. Such theorizing temporarily rescues him from personal despair, but by the novel's end he returns to an actual amphitheater, his faith in the possibility of relationships restored.[2]

The widowed Berners is "a monk for medicine. But a father" (*SD*, 11), whose grown son, Raoul, has repudiated him and, Berners fears, by a lengthy fast is repudiating life itself. Powerless to help his son, Berners joins a parents' group, the "son-blasted, daughter-bitten Society of the Child" (*SD*, 13); what he hears there only deepens his conviction that personal relationships are untenable. After learning of their similar experiences and of reports of undiagnosed deaths of middle-aged parents in Chinatown, Berners comes to believe in what he coins "*Parentation*": "The performance of the funeral rites of parents. By—or with—the child" (*SD*, 18–19). His vision quickly turns apocalyptic: "We are participating . . . in the *cacoethes*, or malignant death of the species" (*SD*, 20):

> We may . . . now be finishing the Voyage of the Beagle which Darwin made. Ask ourselves, he says—*Have* the fittest survived? Or is this nature's quick "Price raised!" for having made that unique life doll, an individual. (*SD*, 21)

Yet even as Berners contemplates a scenario of physical and emotional entrophy, he nonetheless yearns for viable relationships. Throughout the narrative he addresses a series of internalized audiences: Raoul, his idealistic "saint son" (*SD*, 70) on a course of self-purification; a doctor's group trying to discover a physiological cause for the Chinatown deaths; the parents' group, incapable of taking any but the agonized personal view; and, as a kind of Greek chorus, Berners' imagined, internalized amphitheater: "We are the parents and children in a man's life story. . . . We are his Europe. . . . And this adopted country of his" (*SD*, 125). Although he believes himself estranged from all of these groups and what they represent—family, work, his past—his internalizing them as his audiences is, itself, a harbinger of change.

Like the young Darwin on board the *Beagle,* Berners believes that "we must reexamine all human actions, as animal" (*SD*, 23). A post-Freudian, he rejects psychological constructs of human behavior; they are only the "outside of the inside. Understanding people in that way obstructs the natural observation of them" (*SD*, 68–69):

> We are to pretend we are back in the simplest high school biologies, zoologies, being told of . . . how a small arctic rodent, *myodus lemmus* . . . very prolific, makes a remarkable animal migration, to the sea. He asks us kindly to examine—while perhaps holding our breath in analogy—the actions of all *returning* animals. (*SD*, 23)

Berners' horrific vision makes a nightmare of even the most common-place phenomena:

> He used to love crowds. . . . In Europe their prim jostle, the rough marine of them here. But that was when crowds were made of individuals; now the decaying forest smells of the shades that flit it; he hears their blind, seaward motion. (*SD*, 76–77)

The analogy so overwhelms him that "He felt himself lost, swimming between flesh and idea, the connection slipped, yet like a tadpole, he swam because he could" (*SD*, 79). Having despaired of the personal and the psychological, Berners is adrift in, paradoxically, the abstract and the animal.

When, however, Raoul breaks his long silence, Berners begins re-connecting flesh and idea, the personal and theoretical, in a more hopeful perspective. Raoul's enigmatic message—*"Let us be the uncol-lected place"* (*SD*, 114)—is a directive that invigorates Berners as father and, in time, as surgeon. His note is both a farewell and, given the "us," a reaching out to his father. No longer is Raoul "a plummet of stone in the grave of [Berners'] chest" (*SD*, 16), but, rather, a free agent: "whatever Raoul had in his knapsack, it was now his own. Berners said it to himself daily: I will not collect. I will let us be that to each other. At last" (*SD*, 116).

Throughout the novel, hands are a recurring symbol of relationships, emblematic of a painful dichotomy: his own hands, instruments of healing, are nonetheless unable to help Raoul, to touch him physically or metaphorically. Almost as painful is Raoul's scorn for his father's profession. As a result, Berners gave up a vanity practice as a plastic surgeon; even so, "'Raoul didn't care what I was doing. . . . He just thought I was blind crazy to repair flesh.' Let the crockery break, Raoul meant. Let the shards be found" (SD, 80–81).

Raoul's note reinforces the connection between hands and reparation. The note is handwritten, "laid on Japanese paper, with a brush. His son had taken care over them" (SD, 114)—and for that, Berners is grateful. Just as Berners' hands repair flesh, so Raoul has helped heal a relationship by the care and beauty of his handwork.

The same night Berners connects with another child, a black boy asking help for his sick mother. Twice in one evening Berners receives messages from children who want to help, not harm, their parents; hands are the necessary means of communication and direction. But even as they point the way, they point away, seemingly determined to keep their distance: Raoul leaves out his address; the black child, his name.

On the verge of a still more radical shift in perspective, Berners, like so many of Calisher's protagonists, first steps back in time, as though to collect his past selves. Like Pierre Goodman, he revisits his birthplace. The vitality of tradition in Berne, Switzerland, buoys him up: "he had refreshed himself at certain rotundas—his old medical school . . . and the courtyard, eternally rounded in bell and chapel, of the good fathers" (SD, 118). Throughout the novel he juxtaposes religious and secular faiths: brought up as an Evangelical, taught that salvation is not possible through good works, Berners nonetheless had previously sought a kind of salvation in his work as a surgeon. While in Switzerland, "what secretly worries him is what he will do, or his hands or his brain . . . will when confronted with his next piece of [bad flesh]" (SD, 118). The answer lies not in Berne but in a real New York amphitheater where, in the novel's concluding scene, he confronts his deepest fear: "that every hand brought to him will be Raoul's" (SD, 120).

Returning to the surgical amphitheater, Berners hopes his fear will end once, "rubber to skin, his hand touches a hand" (SD, 118). With the patient's before him, Berners' own "hands tremble docilely. Will they work again on flesh? They must decide. He is a returning animal" (SD, 124): not a lemminglike creature but a skilled surgeon. In that moment of uncertainty, Berners recalls a childhood vision of creation: "all of us, falling from our first resurrection ever into the abyss, arched heel over head with our toes in our faces. And outstretched hands"

(*SD*, 126). Looking at the patient's hand—"Bad flesh, good flesh, bit of both" (*SD*, 126)—Berners envisions what acts of creation and of destruction may result. This hand will be

> Ready, if he repairs it, to scatter its chain past anything yet known of, to establish on yet other planets those sad streets that are its synonym. Bringing its dying, murderous seed along with it. (*SD*, 126)

Berners envisions a voyage beyond any Darwin had imagined. Like Guy Callendar's expanded vision in the climactic scene of *Extreme Magic*, Berners' also widens to contemplate and acquiesce to a vast, uncontrollable multiplicity.

Regardless of what follows from his surgery, Berners—teacher, surgeon, father figure—speaks to that younger generation of students: "To give direction. To the next. 'We begin the surgery. . . . Which is a relationship" (*SD*, 127)—comparable to his separating himself from Raoul. The act of destruction is a necessary means of salvation, cutting the bad flesh for the sake of the good: "There are always some who are enchanted with the ministries of life. He calls our attention to them. The Society of the Hand" (*SD*, 127). No longer afraid that "every hand brought to him will be Raoul's (*SD*, 120), Berners "bowed his head, and in his dream, his son annointed it" (*SD*, 127)—a secular priest as necessary to Berners' education as had been those "good fathers of Berne" (*SD*, 127).

While Berners cannot totally repudiate his theory of the human race's inexorable move toward extinction, he is nonetheless "Wary that he might only be transcribing his circumstances—into a general loosening of the hold on life" (*SD*, 116). He no longer needs to see his theory proved or disproved; it is enough—as "median man" (*SD*, 127), the dreamer of the standard dream—that while "Death never fails to move along with him. . . . Hope, the giant mutant, [is] on its other side" (*SD*, 126).

The central characters in one of Calisher's most recent novellas, *Saratoga, Hot*—having similarly coped with extreme circumstances by setting severe limitations on their field of vision—come to the same vitally inconclusive conclusion.

There are unmistakable parallels with *Extreme Magic*, published twenty years earlier: calendars, emblematic of the characters' controlled lives, figure in the opening paragraphs of both works. *Extreme Magic* opens with Guy Callendar gazing at "*The Resourceful Calendar*—for 1846. . . . a tightly integrated little universe" (*EM*, 177); *Saratoga, Hot* opens with a reference to the protagonists' predictable (albeit, nomadic) life. Nola and Tot, a married couple in their early thirties, survive by following the horses: "it makes a calendar, both for the day and the year" (*SH*, 197).

Like Marion and Sligo in *Extreme Magic*, Nola and Tot have a symbiotic relationship in which both are victims, but Tot bears the additional guilt of the physically unscathed. Three years before the narrative begins, Tot was the driver in an accident that permanently crippled Nola, then a college girl he had just met. Tot is burdened not only by guilt but also by the barely-submerged fear that Nola does not want "to live out any calendar. . . . Or rather, since he was driving that day, she will live" (*SH*, 197)—for his sake. Their calendar, then, is a bridge over an emotional abyss neither wants to peer into: better to focus on the sequence of events. On this particular day, however, a series of unexpected events and encounters will disrupt both the day's calendar and the carefully planned scenario of their particular "double dream" (*EM*, 248).

The action takes place in Saratoga, New York, where they have come for the August racing season. This is Tot's world, where only money and horses confer status. At the same time, even the lowly hot walkers, whose job it is to cool down the horses after racing, feel important. Tot belongs to both strata: without money or a horse, he nonetheless has a privileged status by reason of his lineage. Significantly, we never learn his patronymic, only his given name, Tottenham, his mother's illustrious surname and the only one that counts in the horse-racing world. His marginally privileged status is summed up in the name's diminution to "Tot."

Dependent as he and Nola are "on the secondhand largess" (*SH*, 201) of Tot's rich, horsey relatives for both jobs and possessions, they treasure their one month in Saratoga where they can live in their own house, however small, even doll-like. Their world is one of constricted movement and cramped, separate spaces: "the crazy little porch, only doormat wide" (*SH*, 206) is Tot's domain, where, each predawn day, he lists the day's activities "bestride the railing, one foot dangling, and scans left-right, sky and ground, as if the view will open for him" (*SH*, 206); nights, he often perches precariously on the roof, an easy climb from the house's porch. Given the limitations of space and movement, Tot understandably needs "his own porch" (*SH*, 225) and roof. At the same time, they are sentry posts from which he can watch over his prized possessions: his house and Nola. Although Tot regrets Nola's reluctant but all-too-often necessary dependency on him, he nevertheless wants to maintain a delicate balance of mutual dependency.

The tiny living room is Nola's painting studio where, following the few hours at the track spent sketching—all the time she can physically bear—she spends her days painting the pictures that, despite potential buyers, she will store in the attic. Their bedroom is "really her dressing room and just big enough for a double bed, [where] they sleep instead, by her insistence, on separate, less than twin-width beds, since she may wake at any time for a pain pill" (*SH*, 251). Awake or asleep, their lives are defined, joined and partitioned by Nola's physical condition.

As this particular day dawns, Nola and Tot enact what is for him one of the day's most pleasurable rituals: "this once per day" (*SH*, 227), Nola leans on him while descending their rickety front steps. Today, however, a cat, made tame by Nola's attentions, entangles itself in her skirt—as always, a long one to hide her crippled leg. Nola stumbles, Tot catches her: "Is that why the heavy orthopedic shoe shoves out in reflex?" (*SH*, 228), hurling the cat under the wheels of a passing car. Insisting on her right to put it out of its misery, she, unaided, negotiates a descent that Tot anxiously details:

> Brushing him aside, she grasps the railing with both hands. This means swinging the inert leg with the big shoe as a separate weight, which he has never seen her do upright. . . .
>
> So she negotiates the first step. The second step creaks as she lowers herself on it, between cane and railing. That movement, with him ready, she has something done. For the last step, using the cane and a balancing talked of but never dared, she brings herself to the ground. (*SH*, 229)

With one blow of a log, Nola smashes the cat's head, then instantly reverts to her dependent state: "She takes two steps toward him, a third tottering one. He receives her on his chest" (*SH*, 230). "Tottering" back to Tot, to the status quo of mutual dependency, she seemingly negates a demonstrable capacity, physical and emotional, for greater autonomy.

The traumatic episode results in a deliberate break with the day's calendar: Nola announces that this is the one day of the season she will spend the day with Tot at the track. There, Tot once again offers to help her on the uneven ground, but

> she does not cave toward him. She stands, and stands on her own feet, eye to eye. . . . She takes his arm, but almost like any woman. "A house is so—static. Any house. Here—everything moves." (*SH*, 223)

More than a physical achievement, this standing on her own feet—along with the pointed remark about houses—marks a subtle change in their relationship.

At the track, Tot has two unsettling encounters that parallel Nola's more dramatic and physical disruptions of the norm. The first is with a newcomer to the Saratoga scene, Gargiola, whose car had struck the cat. A wealthy man with mob connections, eager to breach Saratoga's closed society, he initially strikes Tot as a Damon Runyon caricature, a lovable gangster with faulty grammar—until Tot notices that "The eyes are not just a character's" (*SH*, 238). Gargiola sees all too well that Nola "'takes things hard'" (*SH*, 237)—too hard: "'Women had ought to scream. My girls scream at any little thing'" (*SH*, 238). Like Lexie, in *On Keeping Women*, Nola keeps things in.

Tot's second encounter is with a very different sort, a Lord Momsey who urges Tot to ride his polo pony in a match. Despite his riding ability and a loverlike admiration for the thoroughbred, Tot refuses: "'I can't risk it. Family matter'" (*SH*, 240). Years earlier, when a riding injury temporarily invalided him, leaving Nola to the care of her alcoholic mother, Tot vowed never again to ride.

These two very different encounters highlight Tot's over-protectiveness and his unconscious, contradictory desire both to deny and to preserve what sets her apart from other women. He does not want to hear her scream as other women do: Nola is a thoroughbred; Tot, her hot walker determined to help her maintain her characteristic calm. At the same time, Tot does not want to acknowledge her infirmity; he cannot bring himself to tell Lord Momsey why he will not ride: "He has never known how to say it" (*SH*, 241).

Tot's desire to blot out Nola's physical problems is clearly evidenced later that day. Before their setting out for a party he presents her with two gifts. The first is an heirloom wedding dress:

> The dress, austere with lace at the top, wild with it below, nestles the long neck, pointed chin and piled hair just as he expected; the skirt hides as he had hoped. . . . But the dress is after all a wedding one, with that double effect—when used for other occasions which such dresses bring. As a sometimes exacting painter of herself, she will have seen that she is aged by wearing it. Yet can she see how behind that double-edged veil the thirties cast, he can still see the girl, in flawed outline? (*SH*, 242)

The second gift completes the disguise: "A slender, cream-colored Parisian walking stick" (*SH*, 242). The maternity shop's salesgirl called it a "'fun accessory'" (*SH*, 242), but Tot intends it to be a veiled necessity, a substitute for Nola's Salvation Army cane. They both know, however, that long after dress and walking stick are retired to her closet, the cane will remain a "fulcrum ever between them" (*SH*, 230).

In the novella's climactic scene, both Tot and Nola are mobilized, thanks to Gargiola who, like Sligo in *Extreme Magic,* smashes glasses and illusions. Arriving home from the party, Tot and Nola find a flower-flooded porch—Gargiola's tribute to Nola's early-morning bravery—and Gargiola himself, suitorlike. He has come to woo Tot's inside knowledge of the track; when he makes the mistake of offering money in exchange for information, Nola intervenes. With so little to give or call her own, she provides the crucial advice free of charge: "'here you build the barn before you build the house'" (*SH,* 262).

In that cramped living room a grateful Gargiola jumps up, breaking one of Nola's treasured champagne glasses. From this point on, however, he is neither a suppliant nor a bull in a china shop. He insists on his right to pay for the glass; furthermore, he wants to buy not one but a whole slew of Nola's paintings, despite her insistence that she make a gift of one. His response—"'So you keep your foot on your husband's neck, huh? Better you scream'" (*SH,* 264)—mobilizes her:

> Dropping the stick to the floor, she has lifted the stoutly framed still life from the mantel and clasped it in front of her. . . . Leaning on the picture as if it is not in midair and not held by herself, she is walking toward that man—not to Tot. . . .
> Gargiola . . . doesn't move. . . .
> He takes it.
> Now she will fall forward on him.
> She stands. (*SH,* 264–65)

Earlier in the narrative we learned that as a child Nola had played a game with her father; he would stand and she would fall into his arms. Ever since her accident she has been Tot's child-wife, tottering toward him. But Gargiola, though a kindly father figure, will not treat her like a child.

Just as Guy Callendar urges Marion to pity herself if she would move forward, so Gargiola jolts Nola out of a self-pitying paralysis. Before falling asleep, she murmurs, "'And the attic—'" (*SH,* 269). She, along with her work, is prepared to leave the confines of a safe space and her paintings will leave the attic for the market place. She contemplates, emotionally and artistically, a wider world: "'And then I'll paint you—' she says in her sleep. 'Over and over. Oh, what a relief it will be. To paint life-size'" (*SH,* 269).

At the moment Nola stood unaided, Tot felt "a peculiar thrill . . . this feeling of separateness" (*SH,* 265) and of liberation. At the novella's close he also contemplates a more normal life: "It occurs to him that with time, passing through the small leeways others allow themselves, he and she may end up like everybody else" (*SH,* 269).

And, just as Nola looks forward to painting life-size, Tot envisions a more active and, at the same time, more grounded life. He wants an end to their nomadic existence: "Waiting for the horses he wouldn't want to be without, but not following them" (*SH*, 269): "Maybe he can get a horse now" (*SH*, 270).

The novella opens with Tot straddling his porch's railing; at its close he climbs up only to slide off the roof—"He always wanted to" (*SH*, 272). Like Nola's taking those few, unassisted steps, Tot's descent from the heights marks a crucial moment of transition from stasis to motion. Soon, he will be straddling—and, no doubt, occasionally falling from—horses.

Throughout the novella there are echoes of another drama of growth and change, Ibsen's *A Doll's House*. Long before Gargiola says to Nola, "'You're—a doll'" (*SH*, 262), the connection has been made, beginning with Tot's and Nola's doll-like house and the similarity of their names to Ibsen's Nora and Torvald, who, like Nora and Tot, have been married eight years. Both women are strong-willed yet girlish, especially in their husbands' eyes. The climactic scenes in both works occur after parties for which the women have been costumed by their husbands—Nora, in a Capri peasant girl's dress; Nola, in a wedding gown. Coached by Torwald, Nora performs the tarantella; silently urged on by Tot, Nola performs merely by walking with the aid of a graceful walking stick, as though not a cripple. Both have two decisive encounters with men who seek access, via the women, into their husbands' closed worlds. Both Krogstad and Gargiola, by shattering illusions, are instrumental in forcing the two women to stand on their own.

Calisher's novella does not pale in this comparison; in fact, the opposite may be true. Ibsen's Nora undergoes a jarringly abrupt aboutface—one moment the wheedling child, the next, a doctrinaire suffragette. (Ibsen also had his misgivings, as evidenced in the several versions of the ending.) Calisher's Nola experiences a more complex, more believable transformation, all the more so because no doors slam.

Unlike Ibsen's heroine, the protagonists of *Extreme Magic, Standard Dreaming,* and *Saratoga, Hot* are not escaping but "returning animals" (*SD*, 124). They have come out of long hibernations, out of dead-end enclosures, to face—quietly, without histrionics—the "treacherous glare" (*EM*, 124) of a vital, chance-ridden world:

> So we may be tossed, whipped, made to run our span again like royal interplanetary horses—the sport of Nature, who is king. To which sport we have added hope, and all our proud despairs come of it. (*SD*, 127)

6

Fellow Travelers

The protagonists of two Calisher novels, *Journal from Ellipsia* (1965) and *Mysteries of Motion* (1983), both literally and figuratively travel the greatest distance—thus setting into high relief Calisher's prototypical movement outward into a risk-laden world. Although reviewers have labeled these works science fiction, they ask not "what if" but, rather, explore what it is to be human. The novels chart at once contrasting and complementary journeys: in *Journal from Ellipsia* an extra-terrestrial travels billions of light years to enter the human race; in *Mysteries of Motion* a diverse mix of men and women leaves earth aboard the first civilian space shuttle. The essential voyage in each is psychic rather than physical: "the movement toward each other's mystery is the only life we know" (*MM*, 513).[1]

Journal from Ellipsia's protagonist is a being from the planet Ellipsia who has volunteered for an exchange program; an all-female group from Earth, eager to become Elliptoids divested of individuality, emigrate to Ellipsia. Before leaving, three women become the protagonist's consecutive instructors in what it means to be human.

Most of the novel is the protagonist's "Journal from Ellipsia" (*JE*, 85). This witty, often impassioned essay on the human condition from an enthralled bystander's vantage point is also a record of intellectual and emotional growth divided into roughly four stages: from an infantile dependency to a shaky autonomy.

Eli (so named by one of his mentors) has left a world of essence where elliptoids—genderless, undifferentiated—elide in a perfect harmony of spheres. It is a serene, faintly fascistic world, with echoes of both Plato's *Republic* and Orwell's *1984*. In theory and in syntax, individuality is impossible: "if One of us encounters One of Us, the form of mutual address remains One. . . . One and One are One" (*JE*, 94). All is not, however, a "serene totality" (*JE*, 111). Most elliptoids, furtively yearning for individuality and corporeality, treasure a myth that mirror images that of Platonic wholes separated by the gods. Theirs is

> an angelic myth . . . that a One of us, therefore all Ones, have within them a heavenly bit of gender, of which, under the Oligarchy of One, we are not supposed to know. And which, perhaps, *may be vestigal*. (*JE*, 101)

Many harbor vague dreams of a "fleshly future" (*JE*, 120); some, like Eli—dreaming of maleness—volunteer to become a "*conscious* mutant" (*JE*, 147).

As the narrative begins, Eli has just recently learned (from Marie, the first of his three guides) what, in theory, it means to be human. Although he understands concepts of time, mutability, the senses, emotion, and corporeality, only experience can effect physical change. With his second teacher, Rachel, he achieves a sense of "Right Hereness" (*JE*, 103) and, more important, "I-ness" (*JE*, 99): "that moment when the One rouses from the everslump of curve—and stands up *straight*. When the One becomes: a one" (*JE*, 95).

This moment of angular triumph is short-lived, and, when Rachel deserts him for Ellipsia, Eli undergoes an unexpected initiation into loneliness and radical self-doubt: "Whatever would i do? i felt myself shrinking to the nothing-without-company that the i so often is here" (*JE*, 194). A new and practical dilemma cuts short the encroaching self-pity: How, lacking appendages, to read a face-down letter revealing the whereabouts of Janice, his third mentor? Here, as throughout the novel, Eli mutates in response to physical and emotional necessity: first imagining a human action or emotion before the necessary physical change occurs. Though "not yet a true lunger" (*JE*, 207), Eli figuratively holds his breath, then a physical exhalation rights the letter. For the second time since arriving, he feels newborn: "One gets born here every ten minutes, apparently—whatever one is" (*JE*, 207).

Having read the letter disclosing the whereabouts of Janice, Eli, like many a young explorer, leaves England for America. Flying (under his own power) low enough to read the sign, "HUDSON RIVER," Eli concludes that "Wilderness would be tricky here, being so much of it inside them; it was probable they would label it wherever they could" (*JE*, 241). Soon after encountering Janice, his third teacher, Eli discovers a wilderness within that eludes labeling.

Having passed through a period roughly analogous to childhood with Rachel, Eli goes through a tumultuous pubertylike stage with Janice. His stay with her lasts a symbolically appropriate nine months, during which time the still genderless being approaches maleness. There are echoes of the adolescent Hester Elkin of the autobiographical stories; Eli is like "'a sneeze with no place to go.' . . . *everything* to say, but not yet the furnishment to do it with" (*JE*, 340).

Eli's dilemma is both unique and quintessentially human. He and Janice are heading in opposite directions: she to a genderless, nonindividuated state; he to a gendered selfhood. Still, Eli, emitting a fleshly rosy glow, romanticizes their time together "as a courtship, even a honeymoon. I was mixed-up, of course, but for me, that was progress" (*JE*, 304). The night before they part, the two consummate their relationship the only way possible: "until morning, curve to curve—we leaned" (*JE*, 342). Once alone, Eli sits in a chair bearing Janice's imprint: "To sit is very human. To sit on the imprint of another is the most human of all" (*JE*, 352).

Having graduated from the safe confines of his three mentors' homes, Eli makes his public debut in the novel's climactic scene. In preparation he has mutated to a less alien form: a booklike object entitled "Journal from Ellipsia"—the bulk of the novel up to this point. Before a group of theoretical scientists, residents of a think tank, Eli recounts his initiations into humanness. At his story's end, a group of Elliptoids appears suddenly in the hall and "all down the aisles a One leans with a one" (*JE*, 370). In a run-of-the-mill science fiction novel this would be the anticipated "moment of perfection" (*JE*, 370), the communion of two worlds. Instead, Elliptoids and humans exist the auditorium in riotous panic.

At the novel's close, Eli, having gone into hiding "until enough of the old pallor and intangibility overcame [him], making [him] fit to travel" (*JE*, 374), contemplates the solo journey before him. At once initiate and observer, he is finally content to straddle two modes of existence. He has banished himself from a paradisal world of essence: "The wilderness was all before me—and I was glad that I had come" (*JE*, 375). Someday he may metamorphose into flesh and blood. For the present, however, he plays the "envoy, which has so many meanings, and all of them rightful—an ambassador and a deputy, a dedication, a poem" (*JE*, 374).

Eli's multiple perspective plays off others in the novel. Eli's first mentor, Marie, "a mingy, gray pod of a convert" (*JE*, 162), is doggedly single-minded. Her achievement—the first human to "Ovolve" (*JE*, 155)—has made her not only insufferably smug but also aesthetically unpleasing: "The vanity of an elliptic being is delicately elongated; . . . Marie's bordered on the fatly circular" (*JE*, 162).

In contrast, Rachel is a role model who, like Eli, is loathe to cross over entirely. Her unresolved double perspective manifests itself in a physical mutation: one "great elliptic eye" (*JE*, 189) spans her temples. With this eye she sees Eli, and the sight inspires her to embrace the new while not relinquishing the old: "'Until it dies in One-ness, the I will remember the I. . . . And will record it'" (VE, 190–91).

Eli's third teacher, Janice—like Dante's Beatrice, both guide and unattainable ideal—wants only to be clear of human misery and the burden of personality. Raised Amish, she wants to be clear out of the world. Of all the travelling characters in the novel, she has the least complicated perspective and the simplest expectations: "'Happiness is a total ellipse'" (JE, 345). She yearns for a Whitmanesque cosmic consciousness, but one not possible in this world: "'I—me imperturbable in the world, the universe. But how could . . . anybody be, as long as she still admits the I-me part?'" (JE, 19).

At the other end of the spectrum from Marie, the character of Jack Linhouse repudiates a double perspective. Janice's former lover Linhouse is a classicist, one of the "few mavericks of the word" (JE, 8) in a scientists' think tank. Years before he saw the chasm between the two worlds and chose not to bridge it: "he'd decided to accept the benefits of all this [scientific] magic. . . . [J]ust let them *keep* it magic—to him" (JE, 74). When Eli, at his journal's end, changes from a book-like object to a living being and addresses Linhouse as "Friend," Linhouse's momentary attraction evaporates before a terrified repulsion:

> He could still believe in gods . . . or he could meet with animals strangely cast up by nature's ever-sportive sea. Or in planets swinging in their own carillons above it. . . . But to believe in this other being here. . . . not now, and not that near. (JE, 366)

In contrast, Eli is eager to bestraddle, record and analyze multiple ways of being, conflicting systems of belief. What sets him apart from Calisher's other initiates into "that mystery, yes, that terror" (JE, 242) of human existence is his unalloyed delight in being always in between, a *conscious* mutant" (JE, 147).

Journal from Ellipsia, "'[a] kind of zoological, psychological *Pilgrim's Progress*'" (JF, 223), is a parable of human maturation. At its heart is Eli's discovery that although to be human is to be lonely, to be human is to be a communal animal. Ironically, it is Jack Linhouse who realizes that

> space, if it existed anywhere supremely did so where the hope of the world also rested—in the human head. . . . Space was what was between people. Even better, space was its own inhabitants, its own people. . . . [H]e was one of those who would never be able to see his universe except through his own quotient. . . . *Me peturbe.* (JE, 39)

In *Mysteries of Motion,* a novel published nineteen years after *Journal from Ellipsia,* Calisher combats the Linhousian view that would have science remain magic, at a safe remove from the lay person's consciousness. The novel is also a parable of that vital relationship between physical and psychic space that Linhouse briefly alludes to. In a interview with *The New York Times*'s science editor, Eliot Fremont-Smith, Calisher explains briefly her choice of subject: "Here was the space age going on, and almost everyone I knew relegated it to science fiction, to unreality. But we are moving into space now, and it could revolutionize our life."[2] In the novel, Calisher imbues that space age with a riveting physical and psychological reality.

Her most ambitious novel to date, *Mysteries of Motion* is a 517-page complex weave of plots and consciousnesses. Each of the six main sections plays a variation on the central theme: the mysteries of motion that implicate and complicate individual lives. The novel's very structure repeats the labyrinthine motions the characters make towards one another's mysteries: roughly the first half of the novel is set in the principal characters' pasts, while the second half explores the dynamics among them on board an historic all-civilian space shuttle en route to the first public space habitat.

Like *Journal from Ellipsia,* the novel's form is that of a document containing the life histories of the passengers in Cabin Six. Framing and weaving between those histories is the log book of the journey's chronicler, Thomas Gilpin, editor of an iconoclastic newspaper and long-time lobbyist for the right to space travel: "Everyone must go, if the world is going to leave the world" (*MM,* 23). Thanks to public sentiment, and despite NASA's objections, the *Citizen Courier* purportedly carries over a hundred passengers chosen by lot.

The passengers in Cabin Six are far from ordinary and their selection, anything but random. To recount how they came together gives some sense of how energetically Calisher plays with the mysteries of motion in the novel, even as it sounds like the year's précis of a soap opera. One of the passengers, a business tycoon named Mulenberg, hand picked three others, for very different reasons. He chose Gilpin only to ensure the presence of a woman, Veronica Oliphant—Gilpin's star reporter and (unbeknownst to Mulenberg) his wife in name only—with whom Mulenberg had a brief sexual encounter years before. He has also handpicked a former diplomat to be the habitat's administrator; Wert's primary reason for going is his Iranian wife, Soroya. Still suffering from the effects of torture inflicted under the mullahs' rule, Soroya, now pregnant, has been led to hope that giving birth will be easier in nongravity. Only two remaining passengers were not chosen by Mulenberg: Wolf Lievering, a German-Jewish intellectual, once also Veronica's lover, and Moleson, "Mole" Perdue, son of the NASA admiral in charge of the *Courier* project—and the ship's stowaway.

The novel's first section, "Gilpin's Ride," interweaves the lives of Gilpin, Veronica, Mulenberg, Lievering, and Mole with the events leading up to and including liftoff. Gilpin has constructed a world view from a deeply-felt personal vision. His—unlike Niels Berners' in *Standard Dreaming*—is a buoyant, all-American dream. Raised on one of the smallest inhabitable islands, off New England,

> His boyhood had deeded him the transportational dream which moves nations and every so often ground-shifts the world. . . .
> The dream in the bone is of migration. Scratch below the supposed goal and every man, every nation, is an islander like him: One day—a further shore. (*MM*, 12)

Though a tireless lobbyist for everyone's right to space, Gilpin himself dreads nongravity. In direct addresses to the reader framing the narrative, he ponders the question of gravity in its several dimensions. In the introduction, he contemplates the effects of its absence, having barely managed to endure "Three weeks of cosmic fright" (*MM*, 18)—i.e., gravity-free training. Both Gilpin's name and the section's title call up William Cowper's "The History of John Gilpin": the mock-heroic account of "a linen draper bold" whose horseback ride from London to Edmonton graphically demonstrates the powers of gravity: "And up he got, in haste to ride/ But soon came down again."[3] The oblique reference to this comic work situates both Gilpin and the others' journey in a far from austere and heroic light.

Like Eli in *Journal from Ellipsia* Gilpin is a creature in-between, who now looks at "the still grounded people" with a foreigner's eye—even before liftoff he feels himself

> standing on the borders of their innocence, which is gravitation. That downer-right of their bodies was about to be corrupted in a way which taking to the air within the stratosphere had never done. In a plane, no matter at what speed, a human body still pulled its own weight. The machine intervened for it, bargaining with Earth for motion. But now we can desert into an element where the body can never be quite natural again. (*MM*, 17)

By the narrative's end, Gilpin will have revised his philosophical conclusions: he and his cabin mates will find sustenance in a psychic gravity that binds them closer in spite—or perhaps because—of how greatly they differ from one another.

Of all those on board, Gilpin and Mulenberg seem most unlike each other. For all his high-profile public persona, Gilpin, once bisexual, now asexual, is an ascetic: all his energies fuel his role as "public defender" (*MM*, 16). Mulenberg, on the other hand, thrives on the exercise of power, both in the board- and the bedroom. He first impresses Gilpin—and, therefore, the reader—as the stereotypically unimaginative business man:

> Born with an indifferent sense of direction . . . he early made the pragmatic jump toward pure passenger. . . . He regards this trip as a particularly long one in an advanced kind of plane. (*MM*, 49)

But he is as much a puzzle to himself as he is to others. In the course of the narrative, he radically reevaluates his constricted emotional life:

> Up to now, his forays into self-knowledge have all been one-night stands. . . . Down beneath them is this other tenacious life of the emotions he's been taught to be ashamed of—which he'll feel to the bone to get to. (*MM*, 347)

In contrast to both men is Veronica Oliphant, who, like Calisher, has found, in her writing, sustenance and liberation. In terms of plot, she is a focal character: Gilpin's professional associate and kindred spirit, Mulenberg's obsession, Lievering's one-time student and, for a few hours, wife. Veronica belongs only to herself, however: a born traveler, she, like the protagonist of *The Railway Police*, carries only one bag with necessities and the on-going poem of her life: "Each stanza so far was an era" (*MM*, 147).

There are superficial similarities between Calisher and her character. Physicially, both are tall, dark, and imposing. Both are outside the WASP culture: Veronica by reason of her blackness; Calisher, by her Jewishness. Their essential similarity lies in a passion for language that, for Veronica, amounts to salvation:

> What did she mean by language? Faith, hope and principle? All she knew for sure was that once she'd found it, the act of announcing had been her way out of the wilderness of early being. So that when in days before she'd have sobbed or raged, now instead a rod rose in her, ramming those valves shut. Cry on the page, the rod said. (*MM*, 158)

Calisher's analysis of what compels her to write applies equally to Veronica:

> I was and am . . . a species of human *meta* physically; . . . the recording ones, who must forever confirm reality by making a new piece of it . . .

and by doing so, bring themselves into the line of being, so confirming themselves. (*H*, 37)

The fourth principal character is a man who has long sought not confirmation of, but escape from, a preternaturally aware consciousness. Wolf Lievering—aka, Jacques Cohen—is a German-born Jew in his fifties whose past engulfs him: "his relationship with himself was that of a man who kept a domestic animal which must someday rear and sink its teeth in him—or might not, fooling nobody but him" (*MM*, 172).

His is the guilt of the survivor: as a child, he and his parents escaped Nazi Germany into a comfortable middle-class English life. Ever since, he has felt secondhand: first to the Holocaust but, ultimately, to life itself. An attempt to render tragedy through art, through sonnets about the death of a young cousin trampled to death by an elephant in a zoo, earned him a publisher's deflating comment: "'These poems have no tact'" (*MM*, 167). Lievering gives up any hope of realizing himself through poetry: "The poem was the perfect product of his training. He was secondhand all through" (*MM*, 167).

Nonetheless, Lievering still seeks, through language, a relief from secondhandness when he takes as his own the dead child's name, Jacques Cohen: "This way he could at least keep a connection with what his own life had not yet imposed on him" (*MM*, 172)—firsthand knowledge of tragedy. Yet, even as he wants language to work a kind of magic, he cannot believe in its powers, warning his young aspiring writing student, Veronica, that "'We make nets of language. But the blood always comes through'" (*MM*, 124). Only years later, as an adult, does she understand that "He was in despair. . . . since for him, no language could compete with his early events" (*MM*, 124).

Until his nongravity training, his only escape from tortured memories came in the wake of epileptic attacks, when a physically-induced euphoria engulfed his consciousness. Associating gravity with his guilt-burdened past, Lievering craves nongravity "like a drug which wouldn't end consciousness but give it a rest from being itself" (*MM*, 180). In the tram taking him and other passengers to the shuttle, the silent, charged reunion between Mulenberg and Veronica disturbs him:

> Such scenes have no place here. . . . Out there—it will all be in the present. . . . Can't those two feel the hangar's growing iciness? Gravitation is departing, lifting off the human onus. (*MM*, 187)

It is ironical, then, that Lievering, who desires to escape "the sweaty bumble" (*MM*, 187) of human bonds, undergoes a sudden transformation that prefigures a subsequent communal change. Shortly before liftoff, Lievering proudly displays the identity mark NASA has imprinted on his skin: "the clearly stamped purple blotch just below the thumb. . . . 'But I like having it. The wrist mark'" (*MM*, 194). By luck he escaped the concentration camp and with it, the mark identifying one as a member of a suffering community. Marked now by another brand, Lievering has joined a community not of ghosts but of flesh and blood individuals.

He has a counterpart in Mole Perdue, who also goes by an alias: his name tag reads "Fred Kim," the friend who underwent training on his behalf. Mole plays the part of the all-American boy, a clown, who, unlike Lievering, seems to take nothing seriously. Under the flippancy, though, he also craves life at first hand. To that end, and with the connivance of NASA personnel, he is the shuttle's stowaway. As the son of the admiral in charge, Mole has heard disquieting innuendoes. Too many corners have been cut—there is no backup in case of an aborted docking with the habitat and the crew is decidedly second rate. Out of loyalty to his idol, Gilpin, Mole sees himself as the human backup, gambling that should the shuttle be endangered, his father will rescue his own idol—Mole.

Like Quentin "Bunty" Bronstein, Moleson "Mole" Perdue is a hybrid; his mother is an Austrian Jew, his father, an American black. They make similarly dangerous "leaps" to save those they love: Bunty into the solarium; Mole, into the shuttle. Bunty escapes harm, while Mole, the crew's mascot, pawn, and scapegoat, is indeed *perdu*.

In the lengthiest and most convoluted of the life histories—the habitat's administrator, Wert's—Calisher relates an earthbound version of the drama on board the *Courier.* Just as his section delineates the mysteries of motion that complicated and enriched his life, so the novel as a whole charts the physic gravitations that bring the seven principles into a larger, familial configuration.

Years before as a young diplomat, Wert was drawn into the orbit of a family and a system of beliefs radically different from his own. In large part, his diplomatic success sprang from his ability to establish warm relations while yet remaining firmly attached to "the country behind him." Yet, over an eighteen-year period, he had an intimate, though long-distance relationship with a powerful Iranian, Bakhtiary (Bakh), who, since the day Bakh's entourage of women witnessed the accidental death of Wert's young wife, assumed a parental role toward Wert.

As Wert's section begins, Bakh, now ninety and cancer-ridden and about to marry again, has sent his only son, Manoucher, an Iranian

UN delegate, to deliver a silent, oblique message: it is time for Wert to give up grieving and remarry. In sending Manoucher as his emissary, Bakh is making each of the younger men a bequest of each other. With this realization comes another, larger one about the essential diference between his and Bakh's cultures:

> At home, friendship died when its generation did, but with them, maybe because they had so many more generations to look back on, its obligation rested even heavier on the young. (*MM*, 253)

The climactic scene of Wert's section takes place in the Brooklyn apartment where Bakh's extended family, having fled the mullahs, gather, along with their guest, Wert, to watch the videotaped wedding. Shortly after meeting a young woman, Soroya, Wert realizes that Bakh has handpicked Wert's second wife. Wert's emotions are further complicated by his attraction to another young woman, also named Soroya, the wife of the absent Manoucher. At the scene's end, Manoucher, who had returned to Iran for his father's wedding, has arrived a broken man, literally castrated by the mullahs. Wert leaves with the first Soroya; in time, the second will join him. In his and their eyes husband to both, Wert will replace Manoucher as Bakh's son.

After obeying his country's diplomatic imperatives for twenty years, Wert resigns from the service but continues to play the role of liaison, this time between his bride and her new country. The cliché-ridden abstraction of America as melting pot gives way to another, immediate sense of the mysteries of motion by which the old world, voyaging into the unknown, becomes part of the new:

> They'll penetrate the contradictory life over here . . . the fat land gone nitrate-rich with wells our farmers themselves daren't drink from. . . . Into it they'll insert themselves, arrowheads steelier than are known here, but bazaar people also. . . . Their keys will grow here as these always grow, iron affecting the host soil. (*MM*, 329–30)

The novel's second half returns to the fictional present, recounting the shuttle's aborted docking and its aftermath. Immediately following the failed docking, a fire in the flight deck kills the crew and ends communication with NASA. The other cabins, which may or may not contain other passengers, are automatically sealed. Those in Cabin Six have created a mutual support system: all are in a "Daze. . . . Of—brotherhood" (*MM*, 387).

Six remain—Mole died at the moment the crew attempted to jettison its mysterious cargo (perhaps a nuclear weapon). Cut off, whether by accident or design, they have been orbiting in a physical but not psychic limbo for an indeterminate number of months. Rescue may occur, but they do not live for it. Gilpin, keeper of the log, addresses the reader:

> In one way, we are no longer representative of our planet. Down below, once you get safely past youth's morbid death-interest . . . your invidiously lively rivalries are often what keep you from brooding on your most certain end. But we here have only this everlasting kindness, almost a vice. In which there grows on us the conscious privilege . . . of having been preselected for a companion death. . . . I think of how we will observe endless courtesies to each others' wanings, to the child in us, to the skeleton. (*MM*, 513)

Mysteries of Motion ends, characteristically, with a paean to the voyaging life. Although "death is sure. . . . the longing for the unknown is the lyric reason that holds us in life" (*MM*, 360). Despite its inevitable destination, life has a paradoxical glory for those who embrace the journey itself—unguided, but not alone.

7

"A Transportational Interest"

It seems fitting to round out this discussion of the theme of initiation in Calisher's fiction with two works, very different in style and tone, that celebrate the voyaging life well into old age: an early novella, *The Last Trolley Ride* (1966) and Calisher's most recent novel, *Age* (1987). The thematic movement in these works is not from stasis to mobility or from false to true entries. Rather, the works chart the protagonists' psychic journeyings of forty years. The ambitious, physical journeys they are about to undertake at work's end are inevitable next steps in their lives.

The Last Trolley Ride is a 171-page idyll, which, though sweetly nostalgic, never lapses into sentimentality. Two old men, both named Jim, reminisce to their grandchildren about the long distant past. Reminiscence never occurs for its own sake in Calisher's works, regardless of why her characters think they are reminiscing at the outset. After forty years of small-town life the two Jims, having immersed themselves in their pasts, decide it is time to move on.

Although the novella is related by a grandchild of "*my grandfathers Jim*" (*LTR*, 77), the voice of one, Jim Eck, dominates. Born and raised on a barge that travelled the now defunct Erie Canal system, he, like Eli in *Journal from Ellipsia* (published two years earlier), is a creature of two worlds: "Barge people had their own way of remembering, half land, half water" (*LTR*, 82). Like that cosmic straddler, Jim Eck savors a double perspective—on his adult life in an insular small town in upstate New York, having only visited it as a child:

> By his taste for a freedom outside it and his stubborn wish to be of it, it had neatly returned him almost to the state in which he had left it, a watery young 'un, Sunday scholar in its visitors' pews. . . . [T]he current was bouncy enough, returning him down like a fountain, or a woman, for his help and his chastisement too. (*LTR*, 93)

Both Jim Eck and his British-born World War I friend, Jim Morgan, become more implicated in the town's undercurrents with their growing attraction to a pair of sisters. Emily and Lottie Pardee are also somewhat peripheral figures in the town's eyes, living as they do four miles outside the town's limits. They keep themselves in view by operating a fritters stand in their house. In a scene reminiscent of the eroticized dinner in *Tom Jones,* the sight of the plump Lottie downing one of her fritters mesmerizes Jim Eck:

> "Day old, you're different," she said. "Way I like you best." Then her lips parted softly, so that he saw the gleam on their jello-pink insides; then . . . it was gone, to what pinker recesses he could only imagine—and certainly did. But just before it went down her, the tip of her tongue came out partway to meet it, nothing gross, delicate as anything, indeed not like a bodily flicker, more intelligent. But it was this that got him. (*LTR,* 107)

Both Jims find both sisters attractive: Lottie, all "marshmallow meat" (*LTR,* 103), and Emily, whose "taste would have been like venison" (178). Jim Eck "was struck with the terror of it, and the charm. Two and two—but *which?*—makes four" (*LTR,* 110). (The question will echo, years later, in such disparate works as *Mysteries of Motion* and *The Bobby-Soxer.*) Jim finds his answer in the novel's lengthy central episode, the town's last ride on a never-completed trolley line, soon to be replaced by buses. During that "August voyage, in that arkful of people" (*LTR,* 191), Jim Eck pairs off with Emily; Jim Morgan, with Lottie.

That day's excursion has a more sweeping thematic significance. The trolley ride—lovingly particularized, in all its nuances of changing light and emotions—is an archetypal journey that gives rise to a communal consciousness:

> Deep in its well somewhere, a voice called out, "This is the life!" and another answered, "This *is* life, and a third one said, "Oh, razzmatazz," and none was identified—who speaks in his own voice? (*LTR,* 192)

Even the children knew "they were on the voyage they had all along known they were, the original voyage, *out*" (*LTR,* 174).

Although that last trolley ride is central to the two Jims' memories, another, long-submerged memory surfaces, one that speaks more forcibly to their present. On the eve of that last ride, the then young Jims had invited Riefel, the eighty-year-old man who had single-handedly made his dream of a trolley ride into a reality, to be the town's guest of honor the next day. Instead, Riefel leaves town for the city. In his refusal to stay and become enshrined as a venerable has-been, like his trolley line, the two Jims hear this message: *"See my dust*. It was a transportational interest all right; it could be the supreme one" (*LTR*, 163).

Forty years later, "Old men, old men. And young" (*LTR*, 247), they embrace it as their own. Jim Eck is a widower, bereft of his Emily, "'an ordinary woman. . . . a nonpareil'" (*LTR*, 226); Jim Morgan, a married bachelor ever since his wedding night discovery that Lottie would submit to sex only if rewarded with food. The two resolve to set off on a never-to-be-completed trip around the world. The legacy they leave their grandchildren is not only their past but also, and more important, their celebration of the voyaging life:

> See my dust.
>   *Even from the air,* said my grandfathers, faded
> and gone now.
>   *Even from the air*—you won't learn more. (*LTR*, 248)

There is nothing elegaic about Calisher's novel, *Age*. The title announces the work's compression and dead-on approach to its subject. At the same time, the novel possesses a pared-down elegance, both structurally and stylistically—and a deep-seated resemblance to *The Last Trolley Ride*. Paralleling the two grandfathers Jim, friends of forty years, are Gemma and Rupert, married for over thirty years. They also reminisce, and their voices, like the two Jims, harmoniously blend. As in the earlier work, the reminiscences prove not to be ends in themselves but catalysts for more ambitious, unanticipated travels.

Of all Calisher's works, this is the sparest in terms of structure and story. The first third focuses entirely on Gemma and Rupert; the second introduces complications—another, contrasting couple and a more disquieting presence, Rupert's first wife; the third returns to Gemma and Rupert, alone in their bedroom. Unlike the two Jims, Gemma and Rupert speak not in unison, but separately and to the page; like the two Jims, they speak in stylistically identically voices. Now in their mid-seventies—"He is the poet—who no longer writes much. [She is] the architect—who no longer builds" (*A*, 2)—they agree to "keep an almanac. For company—to the one who survives. To be read by him or [her]—only afterward" (*A*, 3). The voices alternate, each addressing the other yet gravitating to their pasts, before and after marriage, even as they try to steel themselves for the future: "'You must not believe only in *your* death,'" [Rupert] says. 'You must learn to believe in *mine*'" (*A*, 12).

It is a difficult leap: although they "cannot hope to die in absolute yoke" (*A*, 2), they live, from day to day, in an almost symbiotic union and, sexually, in a "delicately fading pleasure-harness" (*A*, 1): "So we reminisce with our flesh—and stretch our limbs toward the present. . . . We are also making gestures against death—only from a vantage nearer than for most" (*A*, 2). Each bears witness, with dismay, to the other's several small "incidents"—black-outs, blank-outs, falls—not yet, however, serious medical "event[s]" (*A*, 15).

In the course of the narrative, emotional incidents and events jolt their lives' delicate balance. The first occurs with the visit of Sherm and Kit, close friends from their early days in Greenwich Village. Theirs is an enduring, but guarded relationship. Sherm has received a kind of acclaim that has eluded Rupert: "*People* magazine had just called him the grand old countryman of American culture"; he also takes a faintly satiric view—"In his small field as an intellectual who manages to be popular, I know of nobody who has been cannier on the anthropology of success there" (*A*, 32).

Unlike Gemma, Kit, "a onetime Village beauty and darling of the poets and painters of her period" (*A*, 33), has lived in her husband's long shadow. And, unlike Gemma, she has definite and limiting notions about age-appropriate behavior: the articles of clothing (Gemma's peasant blouse) that "'we elder women'" (*A*, 37) should put aside, and, more shocking to Kit, the sight of nightclothes tumbled on the bed: "'You don't mean to say—' Kit says, 'Gemma, do you mean to say you and Rupert *still*—?'" (*A*, 38).

Seeing how they each have aged in four years shocks them all: "They have only brought us news of yourselves" (*A*, 35), writes Rupert. They also bring news of Rupert's first wife, Gertrude, who is dying of cancer. In temporary residence at the Plaza Hotel, she is extending the services of her private, traveling hospice to her former crowd. It is her last of many command performances. Gemma and Rupert visit, despite misgivings—"May one ignore the shrewd narcissism of the dying? Or must one skip to it?" (*A*, 63).

The death room scene takes on a serenely surreal air, thanks to the presence of two British nurses, Sister McClellan and Sister Bond, who, gently but firmly, choreograph the brief visit that climaxes with Gertrude's sudden demise. It is, throughout, a resolutely educational experience: "Even though the Sisters bloom with a health pink with optimism, there's a distinct sense of 'you next, we next' in all they do" (*A*, 65). Gemma records her and Rupert's silent rebellion:

I want to say to them—Don't you dare impugn those who are not in your sect. . . . Those of us who, against all your charitableness know we will die a raging, lonely, irreligious death. A single one, whether or not a boon companion exists. (*A*, 76)

Gemma and Rupert come down from the heights of that Plaza Hotel suite into "the world . . . people call real [that] is quivering all around us" (A, 77); there, they learn of Sherm's and Kit's deaths from carbon monoxide poisoning. Having known Sherm all these years, Rupert can not believe the deaths were accidental: "What [Sherm] cared about was design. . . . What's courage, what's compromise, to a man whose life is losing its design? And gradually. Which may be the worst" (A, 87).

In the novel's concluding scene, both Gemma and Rupert decide on a radically new design for their lives, deciding individually, then jointly, to leave their comfortable nest: "So much of the world only now and then laps at its edges" (A, 117). Like the eighty-year-old Riefel of *The Last Trolley Ride*, an inner imperative tells them it is time to move on. Rupert has bought land bordering a river, close to the farm he "sold in exchange for family life" (A, 77); Gemma has bought plane tickets to Saudi Arabia, where her daughter is soon to give birth to the first grandchild. Most significantly, both are working again: Rupert is writing poems, on Gemma's word processor, and, using Rupert's pencils, Gemma will design their new house. In a passage that recalls Nora's resolution, in *Saratoga, Hot,* to paint—and live—life size, both resolve to "'use the whole house of ourselves. . . . Not close up room after room in us, and live in one. As old people do. And we must let history in'" (A, 119).

Gemma asks a question whose answer reverberates throughout Calisher's fiction: "Can we go on, in this state of going on?" (A, 80). Rupert has the last words—fitting close to this, and to so many of Calisher's novels—as both drift off to sleep in the bed that, through the long years, has remolded itself to their contours:

> So the blank wall darkens. As we ride toward it.
> Our bed a skiff.
> As any child can see. (A, 121)

8

Calisher's "Monologuing Eye"

Calisher's reviewers invariably dive into the same adjectival pool and surface with a handful of epithets—"Jamesian," "convoluted," "dense," and "elliptical"—when characterizing her distinctive style. Whether admiringly or hostile, they often call attention to Calisher's "fondness for the supersubtle."[1]

Calisher's theme and, with some exceptions, her stories are not in themselves either unique or strange; she herself, in several novels, has called attention to the "single story" (*NY*, 559) always waiting to be told. Perhaps these familiar chords create certain expectations in book reviewers: specifically, a realistic, middle-of-the-road style—as opposed to a difficult, self-referential style—as the appropriate vehicle for her theme and stories.

To separate style and subject is to ignore or deny Calisher's achievement as a writer. Her ideal, one realized in work after work, is what she has defined as the "best style": "so much the fused sense of all its elements that it cannot be uncompounded—how-you-say-what-you-say, so forever married that no man can put it asunder" (*H*, 41). To try, then, to divorce the two is to misread Calisher. She is not a failed realist, an older generation's would-be Anne Tyler; neither is she a second-rate post-modernist, stumbling in Joyce's footsteps. Rather, she is an energetic observer of the phenomenal world, making that keenly self-conscious observing her primary subject matter. We are never under the illusion that the world she creates is comparable to an Andrew Wyeth painting, its curtains blowing photographically correct. Instead, throughout her work, the "monologuing eye" (*FE*, 360) tirelessly observes and articulates experience through the filter of a distinctive consciousness.

To grasp Calisher's style it is essential to consider that angle of vision and that voice in direct relation to the theme of her life's work. Just as Calisher's characters, in so many variations, repudiate a predictably linear progression through life, come to reject dwarfing the world to a speciously manageable reality, so Calisher insists on "try [ing] for the life" (*SH*). She leaves it to others to reaffirm a received reality, choosing instead to take soundings on a world that is always in flux. Calisher's style is indeed oftentimes "convoluted," "dense," and elliptical"—so, too, is her experience of the world. In "Short Note on a Long Subject: Henry James," Calisher could just as easily be describing her own work—and its critical reception—when describing James' "extraordinary affirmation of human consciousness. Here, James never for a moment underestimated the intelligence of his readers. There are some who will never forgive him for it."[2]

In a recent *Paris Review* interview, Calisher reveals how deeply she is drawn to a nonlinear reality:

> In Hugo is maybe where I learned the freedom to be discursive, to trust that there will be readers who can accept long sentences, and long meanings. . . . And also accept that a big novel can ramble structurally, and maybe should. It's the run-of-the-mill jobs where you always know where you're going. A big novel has a deeper directional sense.[3]

Indeed, the same can be said of Calisher's shorter novels as well. None of them are dismissable as "run-of-the-mill jobs"; all of them, as Calisher said of *Saratoga, Hot*'s "little novels," "try for more than the short moments of a life" in a deeper, multi-directional sense that leaves many reviewers stubbornly, petulantly, shore-bound.

Calisher's first stories are richly detailed narratives that invariably culminate in an expressible epiphany. The narrator is usually identifiable as the grown protagonist who, possessing the necessary distance, evaluates and sums up a childhood experience. While Calisher's word choice and metaphors are often startlingly and aptly out of the ordinary, there are no troubling lacunae. The opening paragraph of Calisher's first published story, "The Middle Drawer," in which the adult Hester steels herself to unlock her recently deceased mother's drawer, is typical:

> The drawer was always kept locked. In a household where the tangled rubbish of existence had collected on surfaces like a scurf . . . it had been a permanent cell—rather like, Hester thought wryly, the genre that is carried over from one generation to the other. Now, holding the small, square, indelibly known key in her hand, she shrank before it, reluctant to perform the blasphemy that the living must inevitably perpetrate on the possessions of the dead. There [was] . . . only the painful reiteration of her mother's personality and the power it had held over her own, which would rise—an emanation, a mist, that she herself had long since shredded away, parted, and escaped. (*CS,* 289)

In light of the narrative that follows, the paragraph clearly functions as both introduction and summation. The second sentence introduces an image that, slightly changed, dominates the ending. The closing sentence approaches a kind of thesis statement—with, however, one small but significant difference: Hester discovers, in the course of her reminiscence, that she has *not* escaped that powerful personality. There is also a compact framing of the narrative: in the first paragraph Hester holds the key to her mother's locked drawer; in the closing paragraph she finally opens it.

It is not surprising that over an eight-year period *The New Yorker* published nine Calisher stories: each one expertly constructed and radiating a sensibility acutely attuned to nuances of scene and character. Calisher could certainly have continued to write many more such stories: her powers of observation and expression are formidable. But looking back from the perspective of her later fictions, it is equally clear why Calisher moved on, having clearly mastered the demands of the well-made short story, into deeper, murkier regions.

In *Herself* Calisher recalls a writer friend's questioning her shortly after *False Entry* was published: "Was it necessary for it to be written through a man? 'Oh yes—' I flash back, from depths that surprise me, 'you see—he had to be able to go anywhere'" (*H*, 117)—including, it would seem, far beyond the confines of Calisher's childhood memories and the sedate architecture of a *New Yorker* short story. Calisher inaugurated a new decade, the sixties, with her first novel, *False Entry*. With its greater range of expression, its impressive structure, it embodies Calisher's determination to travel on as a writer. She has not discarded the elegant phrasing so characteristic of the stories, as demonstrated in Pierre Goodman's explication of his false entries:

> In each little world I remained for a time, trailing my mists but warmed, always in the end moving on. There were times when I merely "visited" as it were for an evening, dipping into some environment that teased me to know it casually, satisfied to stay there like some tourist with a personal introduction he never disclosed. . . . (*FE*, 395)

What most obviously distinguishes this from the style of the short stories is the dominance of metaphor. In the stories one would expect Calisher to then describe in concrete terms Pierre Goodman's strategies of false entry. Instead, more metaphor-as-explanation follows:

> For more complicated excursions . . . I rehearsed my disguises more thoroughly, sinking myself well in the role beforehand, like an actor with a two-hour makeup to apply. Such wigs and grease paints as I used were of course always "mental"; as I saw how, when skillfully applied, the barest hints furnished me by memory and predilection could turn into life-size

effects, I began to appreciate, in the true spectrum of their possibilities, all the delicately japanned pigments of the mind. (*FE*, 395–96)

The essential difference between the early stories and *False Entry*, as well as many subsequent novels and novellas, is the presence of a narrator/protagonist acting and analyzing in the present. The narrator of the autobiographical stories knows what to make of her past; each narrative generally focuses on one significant incident that results in Hester's learning something about herself and the world. *False Entry*, in contrast, explores the process of making sense of oneself in the world and, more important, of self-consciously acting as both the narrator and the protagonist of one's own necessarily inconclusive story. Permeating the novel is a vital dynamic between the self and the world, a dynamic that Calisher eloquently sums up in one of Pierre Goodman's seemingly casual musings:

> Now that the heat of the day was over, the caretaker was mowing the green space between this wall and his cottage. . . . This was all the mirror reflected when one drew near it—once again the world outside on at its passions and completions, once again the inner, monologuing eye. (*FE*, 360)

Later in the narrative, Pierre Goodman comes to a climactic realization that, in subsequent works, is a given from the very outset:

> Once I had prayed for the intercession of that feeling which wells from a heart that does not pause to know it has it. Now came to me . . . that the heart doomed to watch itself feel is not less worthy. (*FE*, 445)

Considering the novels that Calisher would go on to write, one could argue that such a heart is demonstrably *more* worthy: more acutely attuned to the shiftiness of the self's identity and the world's, more expert at finding the metaphors and similes—as opposed to straightforward description or narration—to render faithfully the experience of that shiftiness. The main reason, surely, why Calisher's second novel, *Textures of Life*, published three years later, is so uncharacteristically conventional and straightforward, stylistically and narratively, is the absence of such a consciousness.

The very mixed reviews of *False Entry* lead one to speculate that Calisher may have retreated to safer, higher ground, structurally and stylistically—only to strike out for the depths in her third novel, *Journal from Ellipsia*, published three years later. In his review of the novel, Anthony Burgess complains that the characters were "too Calisherianly articulate."[4] Burgess pinpoints what is one of Calisher's great strengths as a novelist—unless, that is, the reader insists she adhere to an everyday, conversational level of sentence structure and diction she obviously eschews. *Journal from Ellipsia* is not only a parable of human development; it is also, given its narrator/protagonist's double perspective, an extended, expansive meditation on the physical and the metaphysical, as evidenced in Eli's first musings on the human condition. It is, appropriately, a meditation on quintessentially human movements:

> On, on, on and on, *on;* and on, and on, on. The paradox about distance is that quite as much philosophy adheres to a short piece of it as to a long. A being capable of setting theoretical limits to its universe has already been caught in the act of extending it. The merest cherub in the streets here, provided he has a thumbnail—and he usually has ten—does this every day. He may grow up to be one of the fuzzicists, able to conceive that space is curved, but essentially—that is, *elliptically*—he does nothing about it. He lives on, in his rare, rectilinear world of north-south gardens, east-west religions, up-and-down monuments and explosions, plus a blindly variable sort of shifting about which he claims to have perfected through his centuries, thinks very highly of, and, is rather pretty in its way and even its name: *free wall*—a kind of generalized travel-bureaudom of "across." It follows that most of his troubles are those of a partially yet imperfectly curved being who is still trying to keep to the straight-and-narrow—and most of his fantasies also. His highest aspiration is, quite naturally, "to get a-Round"; his newest, to get Out. (*JE,* 89)

This is one of Eli's more staid, essayistic monologues, despite the rhythmic play in the first sentence and the occasional, telling puns that reveal a distinctive, even contrary perspective: clear-headed, objective physicists emerge as "fuzzicists"; free will has its literal comeuppance in "free wall." Throughout the novel, similar punning occurs when Eli's experiences collide with his built-in computer's input and, via puns, he merges two often conflicting versions of the world.

It is difficult to sum up the novel's style—or, rather, since so much of it is related to Eli—his voice. Encompassing as it does modes and genres, from the most prosaic and abstract to the most poetic and incantatory, it could be termed "encyclopedic." *Journal from Ellipsia* is the first of Calisher's novels to which one can apply her 1969 assessment of Isabel Bolton and the Virginia Woolf of *Between the Acts:* "'But isn't this poetry?' it was said, and the next instant—because a strong analytic intellect, prosaic enough when it wished, was working there—'But isn't this essay?'" (*H,* 297). One of the more difficult passages to label, stylistically, describes Eli's first experience of falling—through a skylight. Not for the first time, Eli's inner computer proves inadequate when processing physical realities but Eli uses all the newly-mastered symbols at his disposal:

> How does one ever render the *mise en scene* here? By what dots ....or symbols ...$+-x-=X-+x-$...by what loci, foci, axis transverse or conjugate can one describe and total it?
> O Appolonius of Perga, who first named Our curve, O Great Geometer! How shall I render a what-where-who-how which is always happening all at the same different ONCE!
> O pi in the sky $----------------------$!
> OOOOOOOOOOOOOOOOOOOOOOOOOOOOOOOOOOOOOOOOOO
> (*JE*, 183)

A superficial comparison between *Journal from Ellipsia* and *The New Yorkers* (published four years later) might lead one to conclude that Calisher beat a hasty retreat from the verbal antics that permeate *Journal from Ellipsia*. In many ways *The New Yorkers* hearkens back to its companion novel, *False Entry,* a similarly long, leisurely narrative. Structurally and stylistically, however, a "deeper directional sense" prevails in Calisher's fourth novel. The earlier novel dramatizes one consciousness. *Journal from Ellipsia* contrasts without intermingling two consciousnesses, Eli's and that of the resolutely earth-bound Jack Linhouse. *The New Yorkers* juxtaposes a far more contrasting, yet more deeply implicated, group: Judge and Ruth Mannix, Edwin Halecksy, and, from beyond the grave, Mirriam Mannix.

The novel opens in a deceptively traditional vein: a leisurely description of the Mannix house, followed by a post-banquet conversation between Judge Mannix and an old friend. The episode of Mirriam's death rends both the fabric of her family's life and any expectation of a conventional narrative. Following that violent death, the novel departs, structurally and stylistically, from an expectable pattern, straightforward chronology being the first to drop by the wayside. More important, as befitting the Judge's retreat from public life, the language itself becomes more richly metaphoric as he attempts to grasp the radical change in his life:

> The floors of his house were well tended. He watched, while a great tooth splintered the parquet and grew upward, then another and another, until he was surrounded by them entirely, and the house, utterly rent by them, hung on its own transfixion, curiously stable to the idling wind. Though he could see the house like that—as if from the air above the city—nothing of the city, or of men alone, had sown them. These were the stalagmites of pure accident, in whose unearthly air he now must learn to live. (*NY,* 59)

Just as the language becomes more complex, so, too, does the narrative perspective. The third person point of view, often centering on, sometimes hovering above, the Judge's consciousness and, briefly, on Edwin Halecksy's, is twice supplanted by impassioned first person narratives: the dead Mirriam as she lives in the Judge's imagination— "I am the daughter, rampant. Built for the sensual light. Seen in it, often by the unsensual" (*NY,* 155)—and Ruth, once she finds her voice. Even the Judge speaks briefly in the first person—in a silent, internalized monologue directed at Edwin.

In *False Entry* Pierre Goodman, by reason of his prodigious memory, bridges past and present and, like Eli, savors a double perspective; the many, disparate perspectives in *The New Yorkers* demonstrate Calisher's avidity for even more angles of vision on the world. And yet, no sooner did Calisher produce her most socially and psychologically expansive novel—one reviewer aptly entitled his review "A Reach for Totality in 'The New Yorkers'"—than she published, in quick succession, three relatively short and quintessentially seventies novels—*Queenie, Eagle Eye,* and *Standard Dreaming*—each with a single, isolated point of view. It is not that the world beyond the confines of the self disappears or even recedes in importance; rather, the individual consciousness as primary arbiter of the reality it inhabits comes to the foreground. As a result, style, more than ever before in Calisher's fiction, equals consciousness.

Queenie and Bunty, both New Yorkers, are of the same generation and social class, but the worlds of their novels are as different as Ellipsia and Earth. Queenie's voice cannot but generate a comic universe in which recitatives—"So, no more La Pasionaria for me? Thaats pop! (*Q,* 268)—are the order of the day; Bunty's voice, in contrast, falls into more somber rhythms: "What are we here for, here for, if not to see each other's lines of force? And see them, see them pitiful?" (*EE,* 248).

Just one year after the publication of *Eagle Eye,* Calisher takes that somber, deeply meditative mode a level deeper in *Standard Dreaming.* The title clues the reader into the distinctiveness of the novel, in which thought takes precedence over action. There is nothing linear about this novel; rather, Berners' thoughts, continuously and painfully revolving around his son, cannot rest in one image, one metaphor, that fixes his son. Instead, he images Raoul in various ways: he is, alternately, a "plummet of stone in the grave of his chest" (*SD,* 16); a cadaver (21); his "still beloved saint" (36); a place to be left alone, "uncollected" (124); and, finally, a priest annointing him as he begins the surgery. In his "Afterward" to Henry James's *The Golden Bowl,* John Halperin discusses briefly the tendency of James's characters to think metaphorically; his conclusion rings true for many of Calisher's protagonists as well:

> Perhaps such an indirect mode of thought is appropriate for people who shrink from direct physical encounters as well as personal and private revelations, people who on the one hand rarely exhibit sensual passion and on the other arrive at knowledge of themselves only after tortuous psychic struggle.[5]

Berners' character is certainly in the throes of a "tortuous psychic struggle." And, in keeping with Berners' obsessional thought and emotion, the prose is more incantatory than in other works:

> We are that animal, which whether it is entering the sea of death or the ark of hope, turns equally to look back on itself. Berners and his son both have dreamed this, that they might run beneath the ark of life and see how it was moving. Along. And many a median man like him. There are always some who are enchanted with the ministries of life. He calls our attention to them. The Society of the Hand. (*SD*, 127)

Calisher ended the seventies with yet another novel of "psychic struggle"; Lexie in *On Keeping Women* also "dream[s] through all the conscious past" (*OKW*, 278) and wakes to chart a new course. Unlike Berners, however, Lexie—in search of her own language—is continuously fusing, metaphorically, thought and action in a "body which acts like mind" (*OKW*, 321)—and vice versa. The interpenetration of body and mind most characterizes Lexie's musings:

> What had these last months been but the greatest of her sullen times? Prison thoughts. . . . Tainted ones. But in the thinking, the prison has disappeared. Glorious thought-careers have surged from behind bars— and oh sages: O Socrates, O Monte Cristo, and who's that female flamenco-politico—O La Pasionaria—I understand how.
> They sprout from the black, barring stripes, in the bright air-float between. Martyrs at their martyrdom have only being—a noose, a fire, a gallows, a blade. Saints at the height of sainthood have only grace. But prison-thought is mortal—boiling headily with all the bloody flux. (*OKW*, 280–81)

Throughout, *On Keeping Women* illustrates the truth of Terence Hawkes' assertion that "Metaphor is not a fanciful embroidery of the facts. It is a way of experiencing the facts"[6] and of giving shape and a kind of permanence to the flits of consciousness that tend to disappear

> down that grotto which is not dream, or sleep or even mind, but exis-

tence-as-record. Which if you persist there will link you honorably to the lives of others. Not merely as one more mortal born to die. . . . In a marriage of record with the world—while you both so do live. (*OKW,* 278)

Calisher's most recent novels, *Mysteries of Motion, The Bobby-Soxer* and *Age* likewise chronicle "marriage[s] of record with the world" in flux. Gilpin's log records the life histories of a group almost as diverse as the bobby-soxer's extended family—while *Age*'s journals project a "single, slightly damaged persona. . . . the Rupert half and the Gemma half" (*A,* 119). All three works are about gravitational attractions—and repulsions—and about the absolute imperative to remain in motion.

From her 1970s novels on, Calisher has couched her transportational theme in language determined to bridge mind and body, the self and the world. In one of Gilpin's earliest addresses to the reader, Calisher reveals, in large part, her gravitation toward *Mysteries of Motion*'s subject matter:

In the movements we make toward one another's mystery, surely there is where life most is. Those ever-shadowy movements—who does not make them, and who is exempt from studying them? But on the *Courier* I would be closest to the nature of motion itself. This is why I and the others, and a great nation, are being drawn there, and why history is. For when people are in thrall to a certain physical motion, then life appears to them to be at its height. Meanwhile, swung like an undercarriage below any large vehicle is that other continuous movement—small, rotor, and fatal— between the people themselves. (*MM,* 44)

In a small-town context, though not on a smaller scale, Calisher's bobby-soxer endeavors to master those "ever-shadowy movements":

Externalize. All the beginning world of it was in my lap and at my eyes, pure and hard in its physical manifestation, only waiting to be sorted and skeined by me, and given back again. What I would be doing with my body and my voice would be a recognition of the world. (*BS,* 93)

And in *Age* Gema and Rupert, "side by side in [their] delicately fading pleasure-harness" (1), contemplate life on the move. Queenie's vitally ambiguous "Ciao" echoes in one of Rupert's last journal entries:

. . .[A]ge isn't at all as I thought it; a menopause of the life principle, a general decline. Or a birthing—by the bodily pain Gemma and I haven't had much of yet—back into the general delivery.

It's like life. A total disease. Or parade . . . Whatever it is, it's worthy of being spoken of every day. (*A,* 112–13)

And in terms as contradictory and various as possible. How else to render faithfully what Judge Mannix realizes at the close of *The New Yorkers,* not for the first or last time in Calisher's fiction: "'life *moves*'" (*NY,* 549).

Calisher has always savored contradictions and dualities. Hester Elkin of the autobiographical stories is the first of many protagonists to experience the necessarily painful pull between mutually exclusive ways of being in the world. In *False Entry,* Pierre Goodman, standing between literal doorways, contemplates, with a pleasure at once intellectual and sensual, "that outdoors-indoors blend which always excited him . . . like the heady admixture of life itself" (*FE,* 261). To be in-between is to be in motion and, thus, fully alive, capable of changes in direction.

On one level, Calisher's own sense of in-betweenness is reflected in her characters' names: her own French first name and Jewish surname that she duplicates, early and late in her fiction—from Hester Elkin and Pierre Goodman through Rachel ("pronounced the French way" (*JE,* 44)) Sinsheimer, one of the three women in *Journal from Ellipsia* to consciously mutate from human to Elliptoid, to Jacques Cohen (like Pierre Goodman, self-christened) of *Mysteries of Motion.* All share their creator's enjoyment, at once aesthetic, intellectual, and sensual, of dualities that keep them in motion.

That same delight with dualities exists at deeper, linguistic and stylistic levels. In her *Paris Review* interview, Calisher talks briefly about

the wonder of the English language. That its words can alternate between rough and soft, harsh and sweet. And, best of all maybe, short and long. Saxon and Latin. Beowulf and Spenser[7]

—or, in other terms, "convoluted" and "elliptical."

On the one hand, Calisher seems bent on explaining and encompassing the self and the world in elegantly attentuated sentences reminiscent of James, Hugo, the Bible. On the other hand, equally representative sentence fragments bespeak a resolutely modern consciousness that is always (literally, it would seem) brought up short by the impossibility of ever really articulating and communicating experience. This distinctive blend of old and new worlds results in an "intimate majesty"—Calisher's characterization of the style of the English novelist, Christina Stead.[8] The style is as paradoxically vital, as inconclusively conclusive, as Calisher's theme.

The "outdoors-indoors blend" that Calisher has known and savored since childhood, from an early awareness of her household's encompassing eras and temperaments, may, in part, explain why it is so difficult to securely "place" her in a literary context. Her subjects—but not her theme—reflect the times she lives in. Her style may straddle eras and genres, yet her voice is distinctly her own. Like Eli's in *Journal from Ellipsia,* it energetically questions what it is to be human:

> What is humane? The small distance. What is wild? The mortal weight. Wherever there is difference, there—is morality. Where there is brute death, here love flits, the shy observer. . . . The wilderness was all before me—and I was glad that I had come. (*JE,* 375)

Just as her protagonists are grounded in the family, in their pasts, even as they journey forth, spinning out new legends, so Calisher's home base has been that transportational theme, "rising always the same, yet never quite" (*BS,* 150), for "the legend never stops, or waits to huddle in one place. . . . It's we who tour" (*BS,* 150). For the reader, as for the two Jims of *The Last Trolley Ride* about to embark on a journey purely for its own sake, "It's all transport. . . . In the first things are the last things; this is the roll of the wheel. Wheel and sail, horse and wing, we are going round—fa la la—the world" (*LTR,* 248).

Notes

Introduction

1. Allan Gurganus, Pamela McCordick, and Mona Simpson, "The Art of Fiction C: Hortense Calisher," *Paris Review* 105 (Winter 1987): 173–74.

2. *Current Biography Yearbook* (New York: H.W. Wilson Co., 1973): 75.

3. Quotations from *Herself* are cited in the text using the following abbreviation: *H: Herself* (New York: Arbor House, 1972)

4. Hortense Calisher, "The Pride and Joy of Growing Up a Woman," *Mademoiselle,* July 1978, 105.

5. Ibid., 105.

6. Ibid., 106.

7. Ibid., 106.

8. "Saturday Review Talks with Hortense Calisher," *Saturday Review,* July/August 1985, 71.

9. Hortense Calisher, "Early Lessons," *New York Times Magazine,* Part 2, 28 April 1985: 38.

10. Roy Newquist, "An Interview with Hortense Calisher," *Writer's Digest* March 1969: 60.

11. Robert Phillips, *Commonweal* 7 May 1976: 318.

12. Eugenie Bolger, *The New Leader* 19 January 1976: 18.

13. Beverly Lowry, *Houston Chronicle* 16 November 1975.

14. Maggie Rennert, *Saturday Review* 46 (26 August 1963): 49.

15. Jean Martin, *Nation* 193 (18 November 1961): 412.

16. Anthony Burgess, *New York Times Book Review* 7 November 1965: 62.

17. Anne Tyler, *The National Observer* 22 November 1975: 3.

18. Doris Grumbach, *New York Times Book Review,* 19 October 1975: 3.

19. Robert Phillips, *Commonweal* 7 May 1976: 317.

20. Granville Hicks, "The Gentle Imposter," *Saturday Review* 28 October 1961: 17.

21. Robert Kiely, *New York Times Book Review* 1 October 1972: 3.

22. Marcelle Thiebaux, *Best Sellers* January 1984: 356.

23. Morris Dickstein, *New York Times Book Review* 30 March 1986: 5.

Chapter 1. Bridging the Gulf: The Autobiographical Stories

1. Quotations from Calisher are cited in the text, using the following abbreviations:
CS: Collected Stories of Hortense Calisher (1975; rpt. New York: Arbor House, 1984)
SH: Saratoga, Hot (Garden City, NY: Doubleday, 1985)

118

2. Randall Jarrell, "The Obscurity of the Poet," *Poetry and the Age* (New York: The Noonday Press, 1972): 12.

Chapter 2. Coming Down From the Heights

1. Quotations from Calisher are cited in the text, using the following abbrevations:
TL: Textures of Life (Boston: Little, Brown, 1963)
Q: Queenie (New York: Arbor House, 1971)
EE: Eagle Eye (New York: Arbor House, 1973)
FE: False Entry (Boston: Little, Brown, 1961)
2. Eliot Fremont-Smith, *New York Times Book Review* 12 May 1963: 5.
3. Donald Jay Grout, *A Short History of Opera,* vol. 1 (New York: Columbia Univ. Press, 1947): 248.
4. *The New Yorker* 12 November 1975: 217.

Chapter 3. False Entries

1. Quotations from Calisher are cited in the text, using the following abbreviation:
NY: The New Yorkers (Boston: Little, Brown, 1969)

Chapter 4. Solo Flights

1. Quotations from Calisher are cited in the text, using the following abbreviations:
RP: The Railway Police and The Last Trolley Ride (Boston: Little Brown, 1966)
ST: Survival Techniques, in *Saratoga, Hot* (Garden City, NY: Doubleday, 1985)
OKW: On Keeping Women (New York: Arbor House, 1977)

Chapter 5. Reentries

1. Quotations from Calisher are cited in the text, using the following abbreviations:
EM: Extreme Magic: A Novella and Other Stories (Boston: Little, Brown, 1964)
SH: Saratoga, Hot (Garden City, NY: Doubleday 1985)
SD: Standard Dreaming (1972; rpt. New York: Arbor House, 1984)
2. In a 1969 Scripps College lecture, "What Novels Are," published three years before *Standard Dreaming,* Calisher reveals the novel's literary antecedent in her précis of Turgenev's *Fathers and Sons:*

> Bazarov's father, retired from practice, but still doctoring, is outmoded in his son's eyes. The sad timidity of the fathers before their critic sons, their sense of failure, of compromise, of not yet being wholly negligible—and this complicated with an insistent love of their critics; opposite them the young men . . . despising their elders for their abdication from it, unaware that they themselves hold the ovum of compromise—and this all complicated with a love for those whom their theories teach them to despise. . . . (*Herself,* 292)

Chapter 6. Fellow Travelers

1. Quotations from Calisher are cited in the text, using the following abbreviations:

MM: Mysteries of Motion (Garden City, NY: Doubleday, 1983)

JE: Journal from Ellipsia (Boston: Little, Brown, 1965)

2. John Wilford Noble, "An Author Thrusts Into the Cosmos," *New York Times* 8 November 1983: C1.

3. William Cowper, "John Gilpin,' *Cowper: Poetical Works,* ed. H. S. Milford, 4th ed. (London: Oxford Univ. Press, 1967): 347.

Chapter 7. A Transportational Interest

1. Quotations from Calisher are cited in the text, using the following abbreviations:

LTR: The Railway Police and the Last Trolley Ride (Boston: Little Brown, 1966)

A: Age (New York: Weidenfeld and Nicolson, 1987)

Chapter 8. Calisher's "Monologuing Eye"

1. *Time* 93 (16 May 1969): 116.

2. Hortense Calisher, "Short Note on a Long Subject: Henry James," *Texas Quarterly* 10 (Summer 1967): 59.

3. Gurganus (see introduction, n. 1), 182.

4. Anthony Burgess, *New York Times Book Review* 7 November 1965: 62.

5. John Halperin, "Afterward," *The Golden Bowl,* by Henry James (New York: World Publishing, 1972): 553.

6. Terence Hawkes, *Metaphor* (London: Methuen, 1977): 39.

7. Gurganus, 169.

8. Hortense Calisher, "Seeking out Christina Stead," in *Encounters,* ed. Kai Erikson (New Haven: Yale University Press, 1989): 91.

Bibliography

Primary Sources

Books

In the Absence of Angels. Boston: Little, Brown, 1951. London: Heinemann, 1953.

False Entry. Boston: Little, Brown, 1961. London: Secker and Warburg, 1962. *Der Endringling*. Translated by Peter Naujack. Munich: R. Piper, 1967.

Tale for the Mirror: A Novella and Other Stories. Boston: Little, Brown, 1962. London: Secker and Warburg, 1963.

Textures of Life. Boston: Little, Brown, 1963. London: Secker and Warburg, 1963.

Extreme Magic: A Novella and Other Stories. Boston: Little, Brown, 1964. London: Secker and Warburg, 1964.

Journal from Ellipsia. Boston: Little, Brown, 1965. London: Secker and Warburg, 1966.

The Railway Police and The Last Trolley Ride. Boston: Little, Brown, 1966.

The New Yorkers. Boston: Little, Brown, 1969. London: Cape, 1970.

Queenie. New York: Arbor House, 1971. London: W. H. Allen, 1973.

Standard Dreaming. 1972. Reprint. New York: Arbor House, 1984. Introduction by Richard Howard.

Herself. New York: Arbor House, 1972.

Eagle Eye. New York: Arbor House, 1973.

The Collected Stories of Hortense Calisher. 1975. Reprint. New York: Arbor House, 1984. Introduced by John Hollander.

On Keeping Women. New York: Arbor House, 1977.

Mysteries of Motion. Garden City, NY: Doubleday, 1983.

Saratoga, Hot. Garden City, NY: Doubleday, 1985.

The Bobby-Soxer. Garden City, NY: Doubleday, 1986.

Age. New York: Weidenfeld & Nicolson, 1987.

Kissing Cousins. New York: Weidenfeld & Nicolson, 1988.

Poems

"The Pear Tree." *Columbia Poetry 1932*. Introduction by Joseph Auslander. New York: Columbia University Press, 1932. 8–16.

"The Young Blasphemer." *Wonders: Writings and Drawings for the Child in Us All*. Edited by Jonathan Cott and Mary Gimbel. New York: Rolling Stone Press, 1980. 105.

Uncollected Stories and Novellas

"The Gig." *Confrontation* 33/34 (Fall/Winter 1986/87): 17–26.

"The Eversham's Willie." *Southwest Review* 72 (Summer 1987): 298–335.

"The Man Who Spat Silver." *Confrontation* 41 (Summer/Fall 1989): 83–88.

"What Country Is This?" *American Short Fiction* 1 (Spring 1991): 105–15.

Essays, Addresses, and Book Reviews

"Reeling, Writing and—Grouping." *The Reporter* 13 (8 Sept. 1955): 37–41. Also in *Herself*.

"Bowlers and Bumbershoots at a Piccadilly Peep Show." *The Reporter* 15 (4 Oct. 1956): 33–36. Also in *Herself*.

"Can There Be an American C. P. Snow?" *The Reporter* 15 (1 Nov. 1956): 39–43.

"Berlin Society Before the Wars." Review of *A Legacy*, by Sybille Bedford. *The Reporter* 16 (7 Mar. 1957): 46–48.

"Where Did She Not Pry, This Great Bee." Review of *Close to Colette—An Intimate Portrait of a Woman of Genius*, by Maurice Goudeket. *The Reporter* 16 (13 June 1957): 40–42. Also in *Herself*.

"Fiction: Some Forms Offshore." Review of *Occasion for Loving*, by Nadime Gordimer, *The Faithful Shepherd*, by Lucette Finas, *10:30 on a Summer Night*, by Marguerite Duras, *Say Nothing*, by James Hanley, *The Serpent and the Rope*, by Raja Rao, *The Tin Drum*, by Gunter Grass, *The Officer Factory*, by Hans Helmutt Kirst. *The Nation* 196 (16 Mar. 1963): 229–32.

Reply to Emily Hahn's "Appreciation." *Wisconsin Studies in Contemporary Literature* 6 (Autumn 1965): 382.

"Will We Get there by Candlelight?" Review of *Inadmissible Evidence* and *A Patriot for Me*, by John Osborne. *The Reporter* 33 (4 Nov. 1965): 38–44. Also in *Herself*.

"The Agony of the Cartoon." Review of *Marat/Sade*. *The Reporter* 34 (27 Jan. 1966): 48–49. Also in *Herself*.

"The Writer: Being and Doing." *American Scholar* 36 (Winter 1966–67): 121–24. Also in *Herself*.

"A Persian Fruitcake." *Status/Diplomat* 18 (Jan. 1967): 33. Also in *Herself*.

"Short Note on a Long Subject: Henry James." *Texas Quarterly* 10 (Summer 1967): 57–59. Also in *Atlantic Brief Lives*. Edited by Louis Kronenberger. Boston: Little, Brown, 1971.

"We've Lost the Art of Friendship." *Saturday Evening Post* 240 (26 Aug. 1967): 10–13.

"A Question of Commitment." [Symposium] *New York Times Book Review* 2 June 1968: 2.

"Speaking of Books: Writing Without Rules." *New York Times Book Review* 7 June 1968: 2. Also in *Herself*.

"A Five-Sense Psyche." *Kenyon Review* 30 (1968): 116–24. Also in *Herself*.

"Civil Rights in Black Hands." *New York Times* 11 Jan. 1969: 32.

"The Big Apple." *Mademoiselle* 69 (May 1969): Also in *Herself*.

What Novels Are. Scripps College Bulletin: The Clark Lecture. Claremont, CA: Scripps College, 1969. Also in *Herself*.

"Mr. Nabokov's Tent." *Triquarterly* Winter 1970: 345–46.

"Women Re: Women." *Mademoiselle* 70 (Feb. 1970): 188. Also in *Herself; Liberation Now! Writings from the Women's Liberation Movement.* Edited by Deborah Babcox and Madeline Belkin. New York: Dell, 1971.

"The House." *Mademoiselle* 73 (June 1971): 144.

Review of *Glory*, by Vladimir Nabokov. *New York Times Book Review* 9 Jan. 1972: 1+.

Review of *Spring Snow* and *Sun and Steel*, by Yukio Mishima. *New York Times Book Review* 12 Nov. 1972: 56+.

"Living in Two Places Shows Us Ourselves." *Vogue* 162 (July 1973): 62.

"Lost Books." *Mademoiselle* 78 (Feb. 1974): 30+.

"Divisex." *New York Times Book Review* 22 Sept. 1974: 47.

"World Violence and the Verbal Arts." *New York Times* 30 Sept. 1975: 37

Review of *The Little Hotel*, by Christina Stead. *New York Times Book Review* 11 May 1975: 6.

"Head for the—Italian—Hills.: *Vogue* 167 (Sept. 1977): 108.

"Twigs." *New York Times* 19 Sept. 1977: 35.

"Pride and Joy of Growing Up a Woman." *Mademoiselle* 84 (July 1978): 105.

"James Gould Cozzens, 1903–1978." *Proceedings of the American Academy and Institute of Arts and Letters.* 2nd series. 31 (1980): 63–67.

"Enclosures: Barbara Pym." *The New Criterion* 1 (Sept. 1982): 53–56.

"William Gerhardie: A Resurrection." *The New Criterion* 1 (Nov. 1982): 46–54.

"Induction of New Members of the Institute by Hortense Calisher, Secretary of the Institute." *Proceedings of the American Academy and Institute of Arts and Letters.* 2nd series. 34 (1983): 11–14.

"Warmth in Chilly London." *New York Times Magazine* (Part 2) 9 Oct. 1983: 30+. Also in *Sophisticated Traveler II: Winter, Love It or Leave It.* Ed. A.M. Rosenthal and Arthur Gelb. New York: Villard Books, 1984.

"Induction of New Members of the Institute by Hortense Calisher, Secretary of the Institute." *Proceedings of the American Academy and Institute of Arts and Letters.* 2nd series. 35 (1984).

"A Family's Effects: The Eternal Room That Is Always Us." *New York Times* 1 Mar. 1984: 19.

"The Reticence of the American Writer." *New York Times Book Review* 20 May 1984: 1+.

"Early Lessons." *New York Times Magazine* (Part 2) 28 Apr. 1985: 34+.

"Reflections in a Writer's Eye." *New York Times Magazine* (Part 2) 9 Nov. 1986: 30.

"Stead." *Yale Review* 76 (Mar. 1987): 169–77. Also in *Encounters.* Kai Erikson, ed. New Haven: Yale, 1989.

"In Praise of Wang Meng." *Nation* 249 (30 Oct. 1989): 500–502.

Other

Best American Short Stories 1981. Edited by Hortense Calisher and Shannon Ravenal. Boston: Houghton Mifflin, 1981. New York: Penguin, 1982.

Secondary Sources

Interviews

Amory, Cleveland. "Trade Winds." *Saturday Review* 54 (8 May 1971): 6.

"Authors and Editors." *Publishers Weekly* 195 (21 Apr. 1969): 19–20.

Breit, Harvey. "Talk with Miss Calisher." *New York Times Book Review* 25 Nov. 1951: 40.

Chandrasekhar, Ashok. "A 'City Bird' in the Suburbs." *New York Times Book Review* 30 Mar. 1986: 5.

Fremont-Smith, Eliot. *New York Times Book Review* 12 May 1963: 5.

Gurganus, Allan, Pamela McCordick, Mona Simpson. "The Art of Fiction C: Hortense Calisher." *The Paris Review* 105 (Winter 1987): 157–87.

Hazard, Eliose Perry. "Eight Fiction Finds." *Saturday Review* 35 (16 Feb. 1952): 17.

"Interview with Hortense Calisher." *The Grain* (Scripps College) 9 May 1969: 33–34.

"New Creative Writers." *Library Journal* 76 (1 Oct. 1951): 1553.

Newquist, Roy. "An Interview with Hortense Calisher." *Writer's Digest* Mar. 1969: 58 +. Also in *Conversations.* Chicago: Rand McNally, 1967.

Pop-Cornis, Marcel. "Convorbire cu prozatorii americani Hortense Calisher si Curtis Harnack" (An Interview with the American prose writers Hortense Calisher and Curtis Harnack). *Orizont* 11 (Mar. 1978): 8. [Romania]

"Saturday Review Talks with Hortense Calisher." *Saturday Review* July/Aug. 1985: 77.

Shenker, Israel. "Hortense Calisher Talks About Writing and Herself." *New York Times* 28 Sept. 1972: 54.

Stanciu, Virgil. "Cu Hortense Calisher si Curtis Harnack despre roman, literatura americana, si contacte culturale internationale" (An interview with Hortense Calisher and Curtis Harnack about the novel, American literature, and International cultural contacts). *Steaua* 4 (Apr. 1978): 24–25. [Romania]

Wilford, John Noble. "An Author Thrusts Into the Cosmo." *New York Times* 8 Nov. 1983: C1 +.

Biographical Articles and General Criticism

Bradbury, Malcolm, et al, ed. *The Penguin Companion to American Literature.* NY: McGraw-Hill, 1971. 51.

Burke, W.J., and Will D. Howe, ed. *American Authors and Books: 1640 to the Present Day.* NY: Crown, 1972. 97.

Evory, Ann, ed. *Contemporary Authors.* New rev series. Detroit: Gale Research, 1981. I, 93.

Gaster, Adrian, ed. *International Authors and Writers Who's Who.* Cambridge: International Biographical Centre, 1977. 155.

Gottesfeld, E. "WLB Biography: Hortense Calisher." *Wilson Library Bulletin* Mar. 1963: 599.

Hahn, Emily. "In Appreciation of Hortense Calisher." *Wisconsin Studies in Contemporary Literature* 6 (Summer 1965): 243–49.

———. "Hortense Calisher." *Contemporary Novelists*. 3rd ed. Ed. James Vinson. NY: St Martin's, 1982. 121–23.

Handley-Taylor, Geoffrey, comp. *Dictionary of International Biography*. London: Dictionary of International Biography, 1966. III, 46.

Hart, James D. *Oxford Companion to American Literature*. 5th ed. NY: Oxford UP, 1983. 118.

"Hortense Calisher Is New PEN President." *New York Times* 31 May 1986: 14.

Kellner, Bruce. *Novelists and Prose Writers*. Ed. James Vinson. NY: St Martin's, 1979. 221–22.

Kirby, David K. "The Princess and the Frog: The Modern American Short Story as Fairy Tale." *Minnesota Review* 4 (Spring 1974): 145–49.

Mainiero, Lina, ed. *American Women Writers*. NY: Frederick Ungar, 1979. I, 285–87.

Matalene, Carolyn. "Hortense Calisher." *Dictionary of Literary Biography: American Novelists Since World War II*. Ed. Jeffrey Helterman and Richard Layman. Detroit: Gale Research, 1978. II, 75–81.

Moritz, Charles, ed. *Current Biography Yearbook 1973*. NY: H.W. Wilson, 1973. 74–77.

Murphy, Christina. *Critical Survey of Short Fiction*. Ed. Frank N. Magill. Englewood Cliffs, NJ: Salem, 1981. III, 1034–40.

Myers, Robin, ed. *A Dictionary of Literature in the English Language from 1940 to 1970*. Oxford: Pergamon, 1978. 53.

Nicholls, Peter, ed. *The Science Fiction Encyclopedia*. Garden City, NY: Doubleday, 1979. 99.

Nyren, Dorothy, et al, comp. *Modern American Literature*. NY: Frederick Ungar, 1976. IV, 85–89.

Peden, William. *The American Short Story: Continuity and Change 1940–1975*. Boston: Houghton Mifflin, 1975. 56–58.

Richardson, Kenneth, ed. *Twentieth Century Writing*. London: Newnes Books, 1969. 105.

Snodgrass, Kathleen. "Hortense Calisher: 'A Beginning Animal.'" *Confrontation* 41 (Summer/Fall 1989): 63–82.

———. "Coming Down from the Heights: Three Novels of Hortense Calisher." *Texas Studies in Literature and Language* 31:4 (Winter 1989): 554–69.

Tuck, Donald H., comp., *The Encyclopedia of Science Fiction and Fantasy Through 1968*. Chicago: Advent, 1974. I, 86.

Wakeman, John, ed. *World Authors 1950–1970*. NY:H.W. Wilson, 1975. 260–62.

Who's Who in America. 42nd ed. Chicago: Marquis's Who's Who, 1982. I, 486.

Who's Who of American Women. 13th ed. Chicago: Marquis's Who's Who, 1983. 119.

The Writer's Dictionary 1984–86. Chicago: St. James, 1983. 150.

Reviews

IN THE ABSENCE OF ANGELS (1951)

Barker, Shirley. *Library Journal* 76 (1 Nov. 1951): 1804.

Beck, Warren. *Chicago Sun Tribune Magazine of Books* 16 Dec. 1951: 3.

The Booklist 48 (15 Jan. 1952): 171.

Buckman, Gertrude. *New York Times Book Review* 18 Nov. 1951: 46.

Hilton, James. *New York Herald Tribune Books* 18 Nov. 1951: 4.

Kirkus Reviews 19 (15 Aug. 1951): 454.

Lee, Charles. *Saturday Review of Literature* 34 (1 Dec. 1951): 37.

Poore, Charles. *New York Times* 3 Nov. 1951: 15.

Time 58 (10 Dec. 1951): 115.

Times Literary Supplement 20 Feb. 1953: 117.

FALSE ENTRY (1961)

Beck, Warren. *Chicago Sun Tribune Magazine of Books* 29 Oct. 1961: 3.

Berriault, Gina. *San Francisco Chronicle* 29 Oct. 1961: 33.

The Booklist 58 (Nov. 1961): 157.

Bowen, Robert O. *National Review* 12 (16 Jan. 1962): 30.

Griffin, Lloyd W. *Library Journal* 86 (1 Oct. 1961): 3298.

Hartt, J.N. *Yale Review* (Winter 1961): 302–303.

Hicks, Granville. *Saturday Review* 44 (28 Oct. 1961): 17.

Johnson, Lucy. *Progressive* Jan. 1962: 49.

Kirkus Reviews 29 (1 Sept. 1961): 810.

Maddocks, Melvin. *Christian Science Monitor* 2 Nov. 1961: 13.

Martin, Jean. *Nation* 193 (18 Nov. 1961): 412.

Morris, Alice S. *New York Times Book Review* 29 Oct. 1961: 4+.

Peterson, Virgilia. *New York Herald Tribune Books* 29 Oct. 1961: 10.

Richardson, Maurice. *The New Statesman* 29 July 1961: 122.

Time 78 (10 Nov. 1961): 102–103.

Times Literary Supplement 27 July 1962: 537.

Virginia Quarterly Review Spring 1961: xli.

TALE FOR THE MIRROR (1962)

The Booklist 59 (1 Dec. 1962): 281.

Bowen, John. *Punch* 5 June 1963: 829–30.

Brophy, Brigid. *The New Statesman* 65 (21 June 1963): 942. Rpt. in *Don't Never Forget: Collected Views and Reviews.* London: Cape, 1966. 159–60.

Davis, Robert Gorham. *New York Times Book Review* 28 Oct. 1962: 5.

Emmanuel, James A. *Books Abroad* Spring 1963: 205.

Frankel, Haskel. *Show* Nov. 1962: 46.

Griffin, Lloyd W. *Library Journal* 87 (1 Oct. 1962): 3466.

Hicks, Granville. *Saturday Review* 45 (27 Oct. 1962): 22.

Levitas, Gloria. *New York Herald Tribune Books* 4 Nov. 1962: 13.

Nordell, Roderick. *Christian Science Monitor* 21 Dec. 1962: 11.

Peden, William. *Virginia Quarterly Review* 39 (Spring 1963): 347–48.

Prescott, Orville. *New York Times* 28 Nov. 1962: 37.

Time 80 (16 Nov. 1962): 98.

Weeks, Edward. *Atlantic* 211 (Jan. 1963): 110.
—. *Survey of Contemporary Literature*. Rev. ed. Ed. Frank Magill. Englewood Cliffs, NJ: Salem, 1977. II, 7386–88.

TEXTURES OF LIFE (1963)

Barrett, William. *Atlantic* 211 (June 1963): 129.
Bemis, Robert. *National Review* 14 (18 June 1963): 500–501.
The Booklist 59 (1 June 1963): 813.
Bradbury, Malcolm. *Punch* 18 Sept. 1963: 433–34.
Brophy, Brigid. *The New Statesman* 66 (13 Sept. 1963): 326. Rpt. in *Don't Never Forget: Collected Views and Reviews*. London: Cape, 1966. 160–62.
Cosmopolitan May 1963: 25.
Francoeur, R.A. *Best Sellers* 23 (15 May 1963): 72.
Griffin, Lloyd W. *Library Journal* 88 (1 Apr. 1963): 1545.
Grumbach, Doris. *Critic* 22 (Aug. 1963): 83.
Hale, Nancy. *New York Times Book Review* 12 May 1963: 5.
Kiely, Robert. *Nation* 196 (25 May 1963): 447.
Lamport, Felicia. *New York Herald Tribune Books* 28 Apr. 1963: 4.
Levine, Paul. *Hudson Review* 16 (Autumn 1963): 458–59.
The New Yorker 39 (4 May 1963): 190.
Newsweek 61 (29 Apr. 1963): 94.
Nordell, Roderick. *Christian Science Monitor* 9 May 1963: B1.
Pickerel, Paul. *Harper's* 226 (June 1963): 106–107.
Prescott, Orville. *New York Times* 29 Apr. 1963: 29.
Rennert, Maggie. *Saturday Review* 46 (24 Aug. 1963): 49.
Sklar, R. *Congress Bi-Weekly* 13 Jan. 1964: 18.
Time 81 (3 May 1963): 112–13.
Times Literary Supplement 4 Oct. 163: 781.
Virginia Quarterly Review Autumn 1963: cxx.
Weeks, Edward. *Atlantic* 211 (June 1963): 129.

EXTREME MAGIC (1964)

Auchincloss, Eve. *New York Review of Books* 2 (25 June 1964): 17.
The Booklist 60 (15 May 1964): 866.
Boroff, David. *Saturday Review* 47 (2 May 1964): 36–37.
Brophy, Brigid. *The New Statesman* 68 (25 Sept. 1964): 450. Rpt. in *Don't Never Forget: Collected Views and Reviews* London: Cape, 1966.
Cosmopolitan May 1964: 10.
Davenport, Guy. *National Review* 4 16 (14 July 1964): 610.
Gentry, C. *San Francisco Chronicle This World Magazine* 28 June 1964: 34.
Griffin, Lloyd W. *Library Journal* 89 (1 Apr. 1964): 1621.
Light, C.M. *Best Sellers* 24 (1 May 1964): 47.
Mannes, Marya. *New York Herald Tribune Book Week* 10 May 1964: 13.

McLeod, A. L. *Books Abroad* 39 (Summer 1965): 350.
Mitchell, Adrien. *New York Times Book Review* 17 May 1964: 4.
The New Yorker 40 (9 May 1964): 194.
Poore, Charles. *New York Times* 28 Apr. 1964: 35.
Sullivan, R. *Chicago Sun Tribune Books Today* 10 May 1964: 8.
Times Literary Supplement 15 Oct. 1964: 933.
Vonckx, A. *Book-of-the-Month-Club News* July 1964: 8.

JOURNAL FROM ELLIPSIA (1965)

Baumbach, Elinor. *Saturday Review* 48 (25 Dec. 1965): 39–40.
The Booklist 62 (1 Nov. 1965): 261.
Burgess, Anthony. *New York Times Book Review* 7 Nov. 1965: 62.
—. *Listener* 75 (21 Apr. 1966): 589.
Davenport, J. *Observer* 24 Apr. 1966: 27.
Griffin, Lloyd W. *Library Journal* 90 (15 Oct. 1965): 4357–58.
Kirkus Reviews 33 (15 Aug. 1965): 854.
Merril, J. *Fantasy and Science Fiction* 34 (Feb. 1968): 52.
Morgan, Edwin. *The New Statesman* 71 (15 Apr. 1966): 545.
Nordberg, R. B. *Best Sellers* 25 (1 Nov. 1965): 294.
Samuels, Charles Thomas. *New York Review of Books* 7 (15 Dec. 1966): 38–39.
Schmidt, Sandra. *Christian Science Monitor* 11 Nov. 1965: 13.
Share, Bernard. *Irish Times* 16 Apr. 1966: 6.
Smith, William James. *Commonweal* 83 (4 Feb. 1966): 540–41.
Time 86 (22 Oct. 1965): 128.
Times Literary Supplement 14 Apr. 1966: 332.

THE RAILWAY POLICE AND THE LAST TROLLEY RIDE (1966)

The Booklist 62 (15 July 1966): 1078.
Capouya, Emile. *New York Herald Tribune Book Week* 1 Jan. 1967: 8.
Cassill, R. V. *New York Times Book Review* 22 May 1966: 4–5.
Choice 3 (Nov. 1966): 768.
Estok, Rita. *Library Journal* 91 (15 May 1966): 2516–17.
Hall, Joan Joffe. *Saturday Review* 49 (18 June 1966): 39–40.
Handlin, Oscar. *Atlantic* 217 (May 1966): 127.
Kirkus Reviews 34 (1 Mar. 1966): 270.
Kitching, Jessie. *Publishers Weekly* 189 (25 Apr. 1966): 119.
Murray, J. J. *Best Sellers* 26 (June 1966): 86.
Peterson, Virgilia. *The Reporter* 35 (17 Nov. 1966): 66–67.
Poore, Charles. *New York Times* 12 May 1966: 47.
Ridley, Clifford A. *National Observer* 5 (8 Aug. 1966): 21.
Sullivan, R. *Chicago Sun Tribune Books Today* 3 (15 May 1966): 7.
Time 87 (6 May 1966): 110.

THE NEW YORKERS (1969)

Anderson, H. T. *Best Sellers* 29 (1 May 1969): 44.

Book Buyer's Guide 72 (April 1969): 51.

The Booklist 65 (15 May 1969): 1163.

Books and Bookmen 15 (Mar. 1970): 26.

Brooks, John. *New York Times Book Review* 13 Apr. 1969: 5.

Capitanchick, Maurice. *Spectator* 224 (17 Jan. 1970): 82.

Choice 6 (Nov. 1969): 1218.

Christian Century 86 (16 Apr. 1969): 520.

Fuller, Edmund. *Wall Street Journal* 173 (9 June 1969): 16.

Guardian Weekly 102 (24 Jan. 1970): 18.

Kirkus Reviews 37 (1 Feb. 1969): 132.

Lehmann-Haupt, Christopher. *New York Times* 18 Apr. 1969: 41.

Magid, Nora. *Kenyon Review* 31 (Winter 1970): 714–15.

Morgan, Edwin. *The Listener* 83 (15 Jan. 1970): 93.

Oates, Joyce Carol. *Hudson Review* 22 (Autumn 1969): 534–35.

Ozick, Cynthia. *Midstream* 15 (Nov. 1969): 77–80.

Publishers Weekly 195 (3 Feb. 1970): 50; 197 (27 Apr. 1970): 80.

Raban, Jonathan. *The New Statesman* 79 (16 Jan. 1970): 89.

Ridley, Clifford A. *National Observer* 14 Apr. 1969: 21.

Time 93 (16 May 1969): 116.

Times Literary Supplement 15 Jan. 1970: 49.

Virginia Quarterly Review 45 (Spring 1969): lxxxviii.

Wadsworth, Carol Eckberg. *Library Journal* 94 (1 Apr. 1969): 1516.

QUEENIE (1971)

American Libraries 2 (June 1971): 645.

The Booklist 67 (15 June 1971): 853.

Books and Bookmen 18 (May 1973): 104.

Davenport, Guy. *National Review* 23 (18 May 1971): 538–39.

Davis, L. J. *Washington Post* 28 Mar. 1971: E5.

Gardner, Marilyn. *Christian Science Monitor* 27 May 1971: 11.

Kirkus Reviews 39 (15 Jan. 1971): 67.

Loprete, N. J. *Best Sellers* 31 (1 May 1971): 67.

McBrien, William. *Library Journal* 96 (15 May 1971): 976.

Observer 18 Feb. 1973: 37.

Publishers Weekly 199 (25 Jan. 1971): 258.

Sayre, Nora. *New York Times Book Review* 28 Mar. 1971: 5.

Spacks, Patricia Meyer. *Hudson Review* 25 (Spring 1972): 163–64.

Yoder Jr., Edwin M. *Harper's* 242 (Mar. 1971): 107.

HERSELF (1972)

STANDARD DREAMING (1972)

Abrahams, William. *Saturday Review* 55 (14 Oct. 1972): 75–76.
Allen, Bruce. *Library Journal* 97 (Aug. 1972): 2573.
The Booklist 69 (15 Oct. 1972): 173 *(SD)*; 1 Dec. 1972: 323 *(H)*.
Choice 9 (Feb. 1973): 1587.
Cooper, A. *Newsweek* 80 (16 Oct. 1972): 110–11.
Frazier, Alexander. *Instructor* 82 (June 1973): 62 *(SD)*.
Freedman, Richard. *Washington Post* 1 Oct. 1972: E9.
Grumbach, Doris. *America* 127 (23 Dec. 1972): 533.
Kahl, Mary Virginia Callcott. *Barnard Alumae* Spring 1973: 22.
Kiely, Robert. *New York Times Book Review* 1 Oct. 1972: 3.
Lehmann-Haupt, Christopher. *New York Times* 9 Nov. 1972: 45.
Murray, Michele. *National Observer* 11 (16 Sept. 1972): 25.
Publishers Weekly 202 (17 July 1972): 112 *(SD)*: 24 July 1972: 70 *(H)*.
Siggins, C. M. *Best Sellers* 32 (15 Oct. 1972): 319.
Virginia Quarterly Review Winter 1973: viii.
Weeks, Edward. *Atlantic* 230 (Oct. 1970): 132–33.

EAGLE EYE (1973)

Adams, Phoebe. *Atlantic* 232 (Nov. 1973): 128.
Allen, Bruce. *Library Journal* 98 (1 Nov. 1973): 2381.
Choice 11 Mar. 1974: 86.
Harlan, Elizabeth Kramon. *Barnard Alumnae* Spring 1974: 29.
Kirkus Reviews 41 (1 Sept. 1973): 982.
Larkin, Joan. *Ms.* 2 (Jan. 1974): 39–40.
Levy, Francis. *New York Times Book Review* 11 Nov. 1973: 38–39.
Liberte 16 (May/June 1974): 105.
Malin, Irving. *The New Republic* 169 (3 Nov. 1973): 423.
McVeigh, T. A. *Best Sellers* 33 (15 Dec. 1973): 423.
The New Yorker 49 (12 Nov. 1973): 217.
Publishers Weekly 204 (3 Sept. 1973): 50.
Stowers, Bonnie. *Nation* 218 (29 June 1974): 829–30.

THE COLLECTED STORIES OF HORTENSE CALISHER (1975)

Allen, Bruce. *Library Journal* 100 (15 Oct. 1975): 1946–47.
American Book Review 1 (Apr. 1978): 4.
Anderson, Bob. *Baton Rouge Sunday Advocate* 27 June 1976: E2.
Bannon, Barbara A. *Publishers Weekly* 208 (1 Sept. 1975): 68.
Beringause, Arthur F. *The Jewish Press* 26 (30 Apr.–6 May 1976): 1.
Bolger, Eugenie. *The New Leader* 19 Jan. 1976: 18–19.

The Booklist 72 (15 Nov. 1975): 431.

Broyard, Anatole. *New York Times* 13 Oct. 1975: 27.

Christian Science Monitor 76 (Aug. 1984): 25.

Grumbach, Doris. *New York T: nes Book Review* 19 Oct. 1975: 3– 4.

Halliday, Mark. *Providence Sunday Journal* 30 Nov. 1975: H30.

Higgins, Eve. *The Indianapolis Star* 18 Jan. 1976: Vii, 11; *Tulsa World* 15 Feb. 1976: 4.

Kirkus Reviews 43 (15 Aug. 1975): 932.

Lowry, Beverly. *Houston Chronicle Zest* 16 Nov. 1975.

McCoy, W. U. *The Sunday Oklahoman Showcase* 23 Nov. 1975.

Mittleman, Leslie B. *Survey of Contemporary Literature*. Rev. ed. Ed. Frank N. Magill. Englewood Cliffs, NJ: Salem Press, 1977. III, 1413–15.

Novak, Michael Paul. *Kansas City Star* 25 Nov. 1975: E6.

Phillips, Robert. *Commonweal* 103 (7 May 1976): 317–18.

Plummer, William. *The Bookletter* 24 Nov. 1975: 14.

Publishers Weekly 225 (24 Feb. 1984): 138.

Rabinowitz, Dorothy. *Saturday Review* 18 Oct. 1975: 17–18.

Rose, Ellen Cronen. *The New Republic* 173 (25 Oct. 1975): 29–30.

Stauffenberg, H. T. *Best Sellers* 35 (Feb. 1976): 335.

Tyler, Anne. *National Observer* 22 Nov. 1975: 21.

—. *Washington Post* 18 Sept. 1977: E3.

ON KEEPING WOMEN (1977)

American Book Review 1 (Apr. 1978): 4.

Antioch Review 36 (Winter 1978): 130.

Bannon, Barbara A. *Publishers Weekly* 212 (26 Sept. 1977): 127.

The Booklist 74 (1 Dec. 1977): 598–99.

Broyard, Anatole. *New York Times Book Review* 23 Oct. 1977: 14.

Christian Century 94 (7 Dec. 1977): 1149.

Flaris, Kathryn. *Magill's Literary Annual 1978*. Vol 2. Ed.

Frank N. Magill, Englewood Cliffs, NJ: Salem Press, 1978. 613–17.

Hildenberger, Miriam. *Best Sellers* 37 (Jan. 1978): 298.

Kirkus Reviews 45 (15 Sept. 1977): 1002.

Leonard, John. *New York Times* 1 Nov. 1977: 35.

Longley, Edna. *Partisan Review* 47 (1980): 308–10.

Penner, Jonathan. *Washington Post Book World* 6 Nov. 1977: E8.

Wiehe, Janet. *Library Journal* 102 (1 Nov. 1977): 2275–76.

MYSTERIES OF MOTION (1983)

Allen, Bruce. *Christian Science Monitor* 76 (18 Jan. 1984): 22.

Bannon, Barbara A. *Publishers Weekly* 224 (16 Sept. 1983): 116–17.

The Booklist 80 (1 Nov. 1983): 397.

Clark, Jeff. *Library Journal* 108 (Nov. 1983): 2261.

Connelly, Sheryl. *Ms.* 13 (July 1984): 30.

Eder, Richard. *The Los Angeles Times Book Review* 9 Oct. 1983: B1.

Fantasy Review 7 (May 1984): 27.

Fry, Robert. *The Grand Rapids Press* 4 Dec. 1983: E3.

Gilliland, Gail. *Philadelphia Inquirer* 1 Jan. 1984: L6.

Goldenberg, Judi. *Richmond News-Leader* 18 Dec. 1983: G5.

Harkness, Don. *Tampa Tribune-Times Commentary* 5 Feb. 1984: 5.

Hogan, Dave. *The Oregonian* 5 Nov. 1983: D5.

Houston, James D. *San Jose Mercury News* 29 Jan. 1984. "Arts and Books," 21.

King, Florence. *Baltimore Sun* 20 Nov. 1983: D14.

Kirkus Reviews 51 (1 Sept. 1983): 964.

Locus Dec. 1983: 9.

Maguire, Gergory. *The Horn Book Magazine* 60 (June 1984): 372–73.

Oates, Joyce Carol. *New York Times Book Review* 6 Nov. 1983: 7 +.

Piercy, Marge. *Washington Post Book World* 31 Dec. 1983: C2.

Schwarzbaum, Lisa. *Detroit News* 25 Dec. 1983: K2.

Stuewe, Paul. *Quill & Quire* 50 (Feb. 1984): 41.

Taylor, Lucy. *Richmond Times-Dispatch* 4 Dec. 1983: G5.

Thiebaux, Marcelle. *Best Sellers* 43 (Jan. 1984): 356.

Tyler, Anne. *USA Today* 4 Nov. 1983: D3.

Virginia Quarterly Review 60 (Spring 1984): 55.

West Coast Review of Books 10 (Jan. 1984): 41.

SARATOGA, HOT (1985)

Allen, Bruce. *Saturday Review* 11 (July/Aug. 1985): 76–77.

The Booklist 81 (15 May 1985): 1293.

Brown, Rosellen. *New York Times Book Review* 26 May 1985: 10.

Elkins, Mary J. *The Miami Herald* 30 June 1985: E7.

Geeslin, Campbell. *People* 24 (5 Aug. 1985): 10.

Hibbert, Dorothy. *The Atlanta Constitution* 9 June 1985: J10.

Kaufman, Kate. *The Grand Rapids Press* 16 June 1985: E5.

Kirkus Reviews 53 (1 Apr. 1985): 288.

Neely, Jessica. *San Francisco Sunday Chronicle* 16 June 1985: 3.

Publishers Weekly 227 (12 Apr. 1985): 87.

Ralph, Phyllis C. *Kansas City Star* 21 July 1985.

Soete, M. *Library Journal* 110 (15 June 1985): 71.

Theodore, Lynn. *St. Louis Post-Dispatch* 12 May 1985: B4.

THE BOBBY-SOXER (1986)

Becker, Alida. *St. Petersburg Times Books Today* 30 Mar. 1986: D6.

Bell, Anne. *Abilene Reporter-News* 25 May 1986: E7.

The Booklist 82 (15 Mar. 1986): 1057.

Buckley, Jeanne. *Library Journal* 15 May 1986.

Dickstein, Morris. *New York Times Book Review* 30 Mar. 1986: 5.

Gess, Denise. *Philadelphia Inquirer* 30 Mar. 1986.

Getty, Sarah. *Sunday Telegram* (Worcester, MA) 30 Mar. 1986: D14.

Goldenberg, Judi. *Richmond News-Leader* 16 Apr. 1986: 15.

Kirkus Reviews 54 (1 Feb. 1986): 140.

Krotz, Joanna L. *The Detroit News* 11 May 1986: B10.

M., E. *Chattanooga Times* 19 Feb. 1986: D4.

Publishers Weekly 229 (7 Feb. 1986): 10.

Riley, Karen. *The Washington Times* 26 Feb. 1986: B4.

Riley, Mary Ann. *Des Moines Sunday Register* 18 May 1986: C5.

Robinson, Evalyne C. *Daily Press* (Newport News, VA): 27 Apr. 1986: 17.

St. Anthony, Jane. *Minneapolis Star and Tribune* 20 Apr. 1986: G10.

Smith, Wendy. *Newsday* 4 Mar. 1986.

Spencer, Mary Ann. *The Blade* (Toledo, OH) 6 Apr. 1986: G6.

Weir, Emily. *Best Sellers* May 1986: 44.

Welborn, Elizabeth. *Chicago Sun-Times* 23 Mar. 1986: 24.

AGE (1987)

Anderson, David. *Journal* (Providence, R.I.) 11 Oct. 1987: I7.

Bauerle, Ruth. *Cleveland Plain Dealer* 18 Oct. 1987: H9.

Becker, Alida. *St. Petersburg Times Books Today* 22 Nov. 1987: D6; *Newsday* (Melville, New York) 25 Nov. 1987: 19.

Belles Lettres 4 (Winter 1989): 7.

Booklist 84 (15 Sept. 1987): 107.

Cook, Bruce. *News* (Van Nuys, Ca.) 8 Nov. 1987.

Diehl, Digby. *Modern Maturity* Oct.–Nov. 1987: 118.

Gazette (Medina, Ohio) 8 Oct. 1987: C6.

Library Journal 112 (Aug. 1987): 138.

Mallon, Thomas. *New York Times Book Review* 18 Oct. 1987: 14.

May, Jeanne. *Detroit Free Press* 15 November 1987.

Rooke, Constance. *Malahat Review* 87 (June 1989): 125.

Wakefield, Richard. *Seattle Times/Seattle Post-Intelligencer* 8 Nov. 1987: L7.

Yuenger, James. *Chicago Tribune* "Tempo" 8 Oct. 1987: 3; *Philadelphia Inquirer* 13 Oct. 1987; *Miami Herald* 15 Nov. 1987: C7.

KISSING COUSINS (1988)

Booklist 15 Sept. 1988: 113.

Dervin, Dan. *The Free Lance-Star* 8 April 1989: 16.

Hoffman, Roy, *New York Times Book Review* 93 (18 Dec. 1988): 23.

Krim, Seymour. *Washington Post Book World* 19 (8 Jan. 1989): 7.

Dissertations

Islas Jr., Arturo. "The Works of Hortense Calisher: On Middle Ground." Stanford, 1971.

Shinn, Thelma J. Wardrop. "A Study of Women Characters in Contemporary American Fiction 1940–1970. Purdue, 1972.

Snodgrass, Kathleen. "Rites of Passage in the Works of Hortense Calisher." Delaware, 1987.

Bibliography

Snodgrass, Kathleen. "Hortense Calisher, A Bibliography, 1948–1986." *Bulletin of Bibliography* 45:1 (Mar. 1988): 40–50.

Index

WITHDRAWN

ALBERTSON COLLEGE OF IDAHO
PS3553.A4.Z87.1993
The fiction of Hortense Calisher /

3 5556 00102616 0

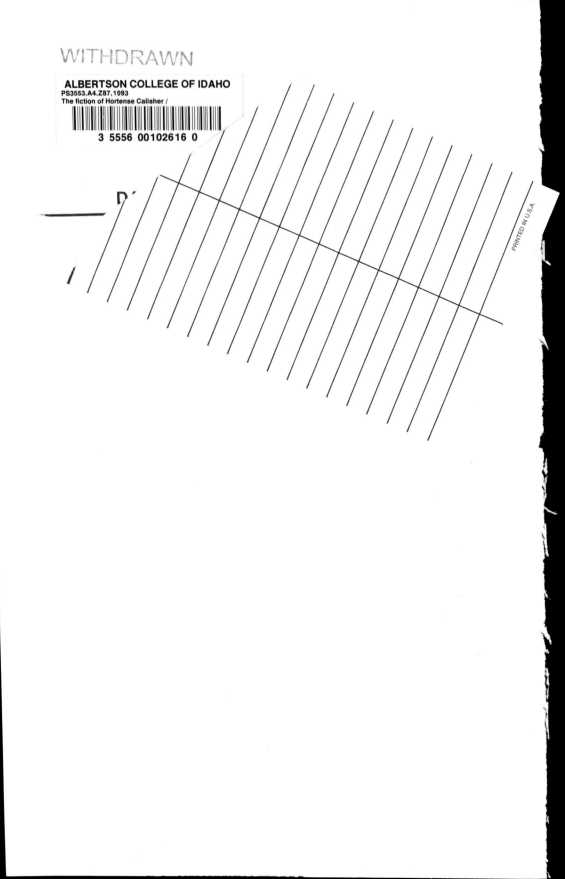

PRINTED IN U.S.A.